"In spite of what many think, Jesus doesn't command us in the Great Commission to teach people all that he commanded us. Instead, he commands us to teach people *to obey* all that he commanded us (Matt. 28:20). And there's a big difference. With this difference in mind, John Frame presents us with an approach to understanding and teaching the Bible that has the goal of not merely transmitting truth from the teacher's mind to the student's mind, but also applying that truth to the student's heart and life. As one of the foremost Christian philosophers and theologians of our day, Frame argues for us to think of theology not only as the accumulation and memorization of doctrinal ideas, but also as the practical application of those ideas to hearts and lives. He calls this approach *triperspectivalism*. Don't let that term throw you. This is a God-centered method for interpreting and teaching the Bible that is deeply rooted in the triune nature of God as Lord and in Jesus as Christ, especially reflected in his three offices as Prophet, Priest, and King. Even though Frame has written much on this topic during his fifty years as a seminary professor, he has once again proved his commitment to help people apply the Bible and theology to real life through this concise and practical book. I know of no more God-honoring, life-transforming approach for understanding and teaching the Word of God than the one that John Frame presents in *Theology in Three Dimensions*. I highly recommend it and pray that God will use it around the world for the sake of the nations."

—**Steve Childers**, President, Pathway Learning;
Associate Professor of Practical Theology, Reformed
Theological Seminary, Orlando

"*Theology in Three Dimensions* is practical, pastoral, and accessible. Need help making sense of what the Bible teaches about our God, our lives, and our world from a thoroughly

D1714338

Trinitarian perspective? Are you looking for a handbook to Dr. Frame's triperspectival approach to theology? You've found it!"

—**Jim Fitzgerald**, Missionary to North Africa and the Middle East, Equipping Pastors International

"This book provides a clear and refreshing explanation of John Frame's insightful approach to studying the Bible (and everything else!) from three different 'perspectives.' It is the fruit of a lifetime of thinking and teaching about the inexhaustible splendor of God himself, God's Word, God's world, and us as creatures made in God's image."

—**Wayne Grudem**, Research Professor of Theology and Biblical Studies, Phoenix Seminary

"I commend this book as a short, useful, practical introduction to triperspectivalism. Frame introduces and explains in a clear way the main triads that he has used, especially the triad for lordship and the triad for ethics. He briefly shows their relation to the Trinity and the way they work in practice. The scope of the discussion makes the book an excellent introduction to the rest of his publications."

—**Vern S. Poythress**, Professor of New Testament Interpretation, Westminster Theological Seminary

"It would be a theological treat to have in a single volume a summary of the chief contribution of arguably the world's leading English-speaking theologian. You hold that book in your hands. John M. Frame and Vern Poythress have written copiously about multiperspectivalism, an invaluable tool in interpreting God's revelation. It is an instance of genuine theological development in that it has no obvious precedent in church history, though, as Frame notes, it harmonizes neatly with the Westminster Confession of Faith. In this book, Frame distills decades of careful Bible study and teaching in furnishing a remarkable key for understanding God's revelation. This is one of those books that you can keep turning to in your life and ministry. The Bible is unchanged and unchanging, but our perspectives on it should deepen and mature over time. Frame shows what these perspectives are and how they work."

—**P. Andrew Sandlin**, Founder and President, Center for Cultural Leadership

"Care. Despite the erudite riches contained in this work, what surfaces throughout is John Frame's care and concern: care for God's glory and for the church. Frame shatters the common notion that profundity and scholarship must be long, tedious, arcane, and impractical. The very structure of this work shows how triperspectivalism is really 'theology as application,' as Frame has insisted for decades—the crisp text, usable discussion questions, handy glossary, and additional resources make this work an accessible and ideal on ramp and gateway for exploring and habituating 'what God's Word requires me to do now,' as John has often put it. Frame cares, and with this work, you can learn to cultivate real care for God, God's creation, and God's image, our neighbors—all to his glory."

—**Jeffery J. Ventrella**, Senior Counsel, Senior Vice-President, Strategic Training, Alliance Defending Freedom

THEOLOGY
IN THREE
DIMENSIONS

THEOLOGY
IN THREE
DIMENSIONS

A GUIDE TO TRIPERSPECTIVALISM
AND ITS SIGNIFICANCE

JOHN M. FRAME

P U B L I S H I N G

P.O. BOX 817 • PHILLIPSBURG • NEW JERSEY 08865-0817

Printed in the United States of America

ISBN 978-1-62995-322-9 (pbk)
ISBN 978-1-62995-323-6 (ePub)
ISBN 978-1-62995-324-3 (Mobi)

Library of Congress Cataloging-in-Publication Data

Names: Frame, John M., 1939- author.
Title: Theology in three dimensions : a guide to triperspectivalism and its significance / John M. Frame.
Description: Phillipsburg : P&R Publishing, 2017. | Includes bibliographical references and index.
Identifiers: LCCN 2017000238| ISBN 9781629953229 (pbk.) | ISBN 9781629953236 (epub) | ISBN 9781629953243 (mobi)
Subjects: LCSH: Christian philosophy. | Christianity--Philosophy. | Knowledge, Theory of (Religion) | Theology. | Philosophical theology.
Classification: LCC BR100 .F6765 2017 | DDC 230.01--dc23
LC record available at https://lccn.loc.gov/2017000238

To Vern Poythress

CONTENTS

FOREWORD

A SHORT, SIMPLE book calls for a short, simple foreword.

Why do so many lay Christians, let alone pastors and theologians, read Frame? Because he strives to be Christ-centered, clear, Bible-driven, humble, and balanced. That's why.

By Christ-centered, I mean that John Frame strives to exalt Christ above all—even above denominations and traditions. Jesus is Lord. He has supremacy in everything. The last paragraph of this book rings that bell loud and clear.

By clear, I mean Frame is a theologian who is accessible to both the trained and the untrained. He is a brilliant scholar, make no mistake about that. But he is read by a wide range of readers who don't get lost when he writes theology. Would that more theologians had this gift!

By Bible-grounded, I mean that he, as a Reformed theologian, is first and foremost a Bible guy. He wants to be faithful to Scripture. He loves the Word of God. He affirms its truthfulness and trustworthiness. He is driven to apply the Bible in everything.

By humble, I mean that both his person and his theological plan ooze with a winsome humility that draws people down that same path.

And by balanced, I mean that there is something spiritually holistic about his theological method.

Which brings me to *Theology in Three Dimensions*. One Saturday morning, after reading some of John's larger writings, I poked my head in his office (both of us are usually at work on Saturdays) and said something like "John, not everyone is going to read your thick theological volumes. I wish they would. But you should consider writing something brief, in book form, on triperspectivalism—something for the layperson. This is something that the church needs!"

Evidently, I wasn't the only person whispering in his ear. Here at last is John's response to our request.

Theology in Three Dimensions is an explanation of a God-centered perspectivalism. It's essentially a way of looking at things—a way of seeing. "Look at it this way," says John. And what he shows us is very helpful.

Now, don't let the word "triperspectivalism" scare you. Triperspectivalism is simply a teaching tool to help us grasp some of the deep things in Scripture. It highlights a pervasive pattern of threefold distinctions, or triads, in the Bible. These perspectives are helpful in knowing God and in knowing ourselves.

So without stealing his thunder, let me tell you why I have found this tool so helpful and needed in the church.

Theology in Three Dimensions, or triperspectivalism,

- Gives me a better knowledge of who God is and how he made us
- Helps me see beyond my own limitations
- Helps us become more teachable
- Is holistic—it speaks to all of who we are, and to all kinds of people
- Is faithfully creative, helping me see a deep pattern that, by God's design, is embedded in things

- Helps me understand the Bible more deeply, knowing its great theme and how it relates to everything
- Helps me teach and preach the Bible more effectively
- Aids my understanding of church history
- Glorifies God and Jesus Christ by highlighting his lordship

Let me elaborate on just one of these, church history, since that is what I often teach.

John believes that this pedagogical tool could actually lead to some breakthroughs in our thinking. I believe he is right, because as I read church history and observe culture, I note that different eras tend to emphasize different dimensions of human nature. One era sees things this way. The next era often reacts against this. In reacting it sometimes even condemns the original action.

For example, take the so-called Enlightenment era that highlighted reason. In reaction to this emphasis on "reason alone," the Romantic movement highlighted feeling and passion. And in reaction to the Romantic era, some European philosophers, such as Nietzsche and the existentialists, emphasized volition, or the will.

Who was right? Could all of them have been on to something important but missed other things because of their limited perspective?

This helps us understand how we can take a good thing, such as the intellect, the emotions, or the will, and overemphasize it. When we focus exclusively on one aspect of our human nature, there will inevitably be a counterreaction that resonates with some other aspect of our humanity.

This also helps me understand Christian ministries. For instance, I'm thinking about the prominent college ministries when I was a university student. Broadly speaking, some college ministries tended to emphasize the mind (InterVarsity), others the will (CRU and the Navigators), still others the emotions (charismatic fellowships). Students would often jump from one group to another when they sensed some yearning to balance out. This little example, I believe, is a microcosm of much of American and British evangelicalism.

Or apply this to the church and seminary world. Some have noted that in Reformed circles, people tend to fall into three groups—the "docts," the "piets," and the "Kuyps." The "docts" tend to prize precise doctrine above all, the "piets" (pietists) emphasize the heart and personal devotion, and the "Kuyps" (Kuyperians) value cultural engagement and transformation.

But again, don't we need all three? Knowing this can not only lessen the tension between these different "camps" but can also help us to avoid the temptation of lopsidedness.

I don't believe John Frame's teaching on triperspectivalism is a fanciful speculation. To the contrary, John is on to something important. He is identifying some deep patterns built into the world by the Creator that are also reflected all over Scripture.

Frame is calling us all to a holistic vision represented in the Great Commandment itself, where we are to love the Lord our God with *all* that we are.

So let John Frame lead you in this little book—to a deeper faith, to a more whole-souled love for Christ, and to a greater appreciation for the diversity of the body of Christ.

Donald W. Sweeting
Former president, Reformed Theological Seminary in Orlando
Current president, Colorado Christian University

PREFACE

OVER MANY YEARS, with the invaluable collaboration of Vern Poythress, to whom I have dedicated this volume, I have argued the value of looking at theological issues from multiple perspectives, particularly a threefold set of perspectives related to the biblical doctrine of the Trinity. People have often asked for a simple introduction to our "triperspectivalism." Some introductory accounts of it do exist, particularly Poythress's *Symphonic Theology*[1] and my "A Primer on Perspectivalism."[2] Larger accounts include his *Philosophy, Science and the Sovereignty of God*,[3] my *DKG* and *PWG*, and some sections within our other books, especially his *Redeeming Philosophy*[4] and my *DG*.[5] I have used many triperspectival formulations in

---

1. Vern S. Poythress, *Symphonic Theology* (Grand Rapids: Zondervan, 1987).

2. John Frame, *SSW1* (Phillipsburg, NJ: P&R Publishing, 2014), 3–18, cf. 19–25.

3. Vern S. Poythress, *Philosophy, Science and the Sovereignty of God* (Nutley, NJ: Presbyterian and Reformed, 1976).

4. Vern S. Poythress, *Redeeming Philosophy: A God-Centered Approach* (Wheaton, IL: Crossway, 2014), 53–134.

5. One appendix in *DG* (A, 743–50) lists 112 threefold distinctions that can conceivably be interpreted triperspectivally—some, to be sure, with tongue in cheek.

my four-volume Theology of Lordship[6] project and in my *ST*. But there seems to be demand for still another introductory work on triperspectivalism: a book under a hundred pages, explaining jargon, emphasizing practicality. That is the task I attempt here, summarizing and updating our past efforts.

Perspectival analyses of theological doctrines can appear very different from more traditional formulations, even those of confessions and creeds. For this reason, many readers worry that we are presenting something novel. I hope this volume will assure those and other readers that my writings and those of Poythress aim to represent and defend Reformed orthodoxy as it is classically presented in the Westminster Confession of Faith. Although our presentations and arguments are sometimes unusual, we almost always come to the same conclusions as those of the Reformed confessions: two routes to the same destination. Why two routes? I hope to show that in the present volume, especially chapter 8, "What to Do with Perspectives."

Triperspectivalism is, in the main, a pedagogical approach, a way of teaching the Bible—that is, doing what theology is supposed to do. Beyond pedagogy, it may help us to get deeper into the doctrine of the Trinity in its implications for our thought and life. I'm sure that nobody thinks we have exhausted those implications in past theology.

I would not be writing this book except for the fact that many of my students and readers over a period of almost fifty years have expressed thanks for a method that has helped their Bible study and therefore has deepened their relationship with God.

My thanks to all who have helped with the publication of this work. My longtime friend John Hughes has again

6. That is, *DKG*, *DG*, *DCL*, and *DWG*.

managed this project from manuscript to release. Thanks to P&R Publishing for accepting this project and for implementing their resources to make it available. Thanks especially to Andrew Buss for his excellent work in copyediting. Thanks also to Don Sweeting, president of Colorado Christian University, who first suggested the project to me.

There is much more to come. My friend Vern Poythress has developed this structure into outlines of the science of linguistics and other sciences. His forthcoming *Knowing and the Trinity: How Perspectives in Human Knowledge Imitate the Trinity*[7] develops the Trinitarian basis of perspectivalism far more deeply than I have been able to do here. Others, like Timothy Miller and Brant Bosserman, are building on this foundation on the assumption that it will yield much fruit for future theology and other fields of study.

I think that at least this approach has the power to integrate a number of biblical teachings and to help us more effectively teach the Word of God. I pray that God will use these principles to make his Word better understood throughout the world.

---

7. Vern S. Poythress, *Knowing and the Trinity: How Perspectives in Human Knowledge Imitate the Trinity* (Phillipsburg, NJ: P&R Publishing, 2018).

ABBREVIATIONS

DCL   John M. Frame, *The Doctrine of the Christian Life*, A Theology of Lordship, vol. 3 (Phillipsburg, NJ: P&R Publishing, 2008)

DG   John M. Frame, *The Doctrine of God*, A Theology of Lordship, vol. 2 (Phillipsburg, NJ: P&R Publishing, 2002)

DKG   John M. Frame, *The Doctrine of the Knowledge of God*, A Theology of Lordship, vol. 1 (Phillipsburg, NJ: Presbyterian and Reformed, 1987)

DWG   John M. Frame, *The Doctrine of the Word of God*, A Theology of Lordship, vol. 4 (Phillipsburg, NJ: P&R Publishing, 2010)

ET   John M. Frame, *The Escondido Theology* (Lakeland, FL: Whitefield Media Productions, 2011)

HWPT   John M. Frame, *A History of Western Philosophy and Theology* (Phillipsburg, NJ: P&R Publishing, 2015)

NT   New Testament

Abbreviations

OT	Old Testament
PWG	John M. Frame, *Perspectives on the Word of God* (Eugene, OR: Wipf & Stock, 1999)
SSW1	John M. Frame, *Selected Shorter Writings, Vol. 1* (Phillipsburg, NJ: P&R Publishing, 2014)
SSW3	John M. Frame, *Selected Shorter Writings, Vol. 3* (Phillipsburg, NJ: P&R Publishing, 2016)
ST	John M. Frame, *Systematic Theology: An Introduction to Christian Belief* (Phillipsburg, NJ: P&R Publishing, 2013)

PERSPECTIVES

TO GIVE A detailed description of a tree, you really need to look at it from all sides. But of course, you can't see all sides at once. You may, therefore, need to do some walking. Your eyes won't be enough. But your eyes and your legs can combine to do a better job.

But even then your description won't be good enough for some purposes. For a *scientific* description, you will need some instruments: tools for a careful dissection, a powerful microscope. For a tree, ordinary as it may be, is a complicated thing. Think of all the veins in the leaves, the rings in the trunk. Think of how the tree brings sunlight, rain, and soil nutrients together to grow as it should. And then think of how each of these processes is itself complex. Today, we like to think that ultimately it reduces to protons and other tiny particles. To describe all of this, we need to look at the tree—not just from north, south, east, and west, but from a truly vast number of perspectives, external and internal.

And there is more. To gain a fuller perspective of the tree, we need to think about more than the tree itself. We also need to think about the tree's relationships with other things: the sun, the atmosphere, the weather, the insects, the bacteria, other trees, and the tree's history as indicated by its rings and the laws of chemistry, biology, and physics. We need to look at the human influence on the breeding of the tree through the centuries and the way this and similar trees have been used in human civilization. Each of these will lead us to indefinite numbers of additional perspectives, enlarging the knowledge available to our present perspective.

Trees appear in many famous artistic creations. They are part of many noted scenes, like the White House Christmas tree lighting and the California redwoods. They play significant roles in history, such as the battering rams used in medieval warfare. Often they take on symbolic significance, as the Tree of Life in the Bible, or the palms used to advertise sunny places. There are many trees we don't understand until we look far beyond their physical properties.

Vern Poythress defines "perspective" as "a view from somewhere. More precisely, it is a (1) view of something (2) by someone (3) from somewhere."[1] A *perspective*, literally, is a position from which a person sees something. It is the standpoint, the angle from which he looks. By extension, the term includes other sensory experience—hearing, taste, touch, and sight—as well as the activities we call reasoning. A person's perspective is the standpoint[2] from which he gains his overall understanding of the world around him. My personal perspective is what I sense around me at the moment when I am using my legs, scientific tools, and the like to get a fuller understanding. Ultimately, all this knowledge comes to me through my own body—through my senses and the

---

1. See Poythress, *Knowing and the Trinity: How Perspectives in Human Knowledge Imitate the Trinity* (Phillipsburg, NJ: P&R Publishing, 2018).

2. The Greek thinker Archimedes is quoted as saying "Give me a place to stand (a *pou sto*) and I shall move the earth." For Archimedes, the *pou sto* gives not only understanding but also power.

operations by which my brain organizes my sense impressions into knowledge.

As we explore the tree in broader and broader contexts, more and more perspectives emerge. We consider the human influence on the breeding of the tree through the centuries and the way this and similar trees have been used in human civilization. Each of these will lead us to indefinite numbers of additional perspectives, enlarging the knowledge available to our present perspective.

So each perspective includes others. My sensory experience includes what I sense from far away as well as what I sense from close up. It includes what I can see from the north and from the south. It includes what I sense through the naked eye and through scientific instruments. These are multiple perspectives, but they all are part of the general personal perspective that constitutes my experience and assessment of the real world.

In one way each person's perspective includes the entire universe, though it is, in a different sense, a small part of the universe. When I stand at night, looking into the sky, I see billions of stars, planets, and other cosmic objects. I don't see them in detail or with absolute clarity. But my visual field has no end. The same is true when I look across the world, into the horizon. There is, again, no limit to my field of vision. I see everything that is visible from my position in space. In one sense I see everything, though not with perfect clarity.

But from another perspective(!) I judge my perspective to be very tiny. In comparison with other people, I know very little. And I am always aware of the limits of what I can perceive and what I can know.

When I meditate on the vastness, and the smallness, of human knowledge, it is natural to compare my knowledge to that of God.

GOD'S PERSPECTIVE

This book deals with Christian theology, and so readers will understand that it presupposes the biblical God. God is the one who made this vastly and beautifully complicated world. Each tree displays his vast wisdom. Jesus said that God sees each sparrow fall (Matt. 10:29), and he knows the number of hairs on our heads (Matt. 10:30). Certainly he also knows every leaf on our tree, every root, every strip of bark.

To understand better the vastness of God's knowledge, we can compare it to our own, but also to the knowledge of animals. I have owned three Pembroke Welsh Corgis through my life, and they have been the smartest dogs alive. I taught them not only to sit, come, stand, and roll over, but also to turn to the right and turn to the left. I taught one of them to respond to dogs and cats on the TV screen (a lesson I eventually came to regret). I am sure that in a post-apocalyptic world a Welsh Corgi could find food for me and my wife better than I could. But my dogs always had one notable level of ignorance: they had no idea what I was writing in my books. They could not read even the first paragraphs of the introductions. Surely the comparison between my dogs' knowledge and my own is similar to the difference between my knowledge and God's. There are items of knowledge that are quite elementary to God that I have no idea of. People who use their reason to figure out the coherence of God's attributes and the reason for God's creation of evil would be like my dog if he had tried to master the first sentence in my *ST*. To his immense credit, he never tried to do that.

Theologians say that because God made everything and remembers what he has made, he is omniscient. But his knowledge includes not only the basic facts about the trees and the hairs and the sparrows. He sees all these things from every possible *perspective*. He sees the sparrow from behind its head as well as in front of its face. And he sees my hair from its follicle to its ever decreasing pigment. He sees it from his omniscient divine perspective, but he also understands fully how my wife experiences my hair. And he is able to see it as anyone else sees it, from every possible vantage point. He knows what the sparrow looks like to another sparrow, or to the hawk soaring overhead. He sees my hair from the vantage point of the fly on the wall of my office. He even knows perspectives that are merely possible: he knows what my hair *would* look like from the vantage point of a fly on the wall, even when there is no fly on my wall. So God is not only omniscient but omniperspectival.

INCORPORATING OTHER HUMAN PERSPECTIVES

As I sit in my office chair, I can look out the window, which conveys a splendid view of the seminary parking lot. That is, it gives me access to a perspective on the lot that comes to me essentially through my eyes. If I were to go outside, that perspective would be enriched by sounds, smells, and things I can touch, along with the intellectual reflections of my brain. That is all part of one perspective—*my* perspective, the perspective accessible by my own body. In one sense, I have only that one perspective on the world. Everything I know, I access through my body. And, as we sometimes say, I can't step outside my own skin.

But learning never ends with my immediate experience. I see George on the parking lot, and I ask him whether his five-year-old boy has recovered from his cold. He tells me yes, and I add that fact to my knowledge of the world. I don't *see* the child, and his health is not part of my *immediate* experience.

But George is part of that, and I trust George's reports of his own immediate experience. So George's knowledge enriches mine. My perspective gets larger by incorporating George's perspective. So, though I cannot step outside my own skin, I can in some ways add the perspectives of others to my own. Of course, I don't trust everybody the way I trust George. And on some matters I might not even fully trust George. The expansion of my perspective is a *critical* task. I have to make judgments about whether and to what extent the perspectives of others are reliable, and to what extent their testimonies about their experience are true. But my critical thoughts are also part of my perspective on the world.

How do I make such judgments? What is the process that enables me to judge to what extent another's perspective is true? To a large extent our judgments in such matters begin with intuition. Some testimony, like George's testimony about his son, seems obviously true. George is a person like me. He has proved himself right in the past. I have not known him to deceive me or to be mistaken about something in his immediate experience. There is no problem with his. And there is the "ring of truth" in what he says. It fits together with the judgments I make about other aspects of my experience. These factors come together harmoniously. They are "intuitive." We just know, because we know what truth sounds like and looks like.

In other cases, however, there are questions to which the answers aren't obvious. Sabrina is a Democrat, and she tells me that we could give a free college education to everyone if we could tax millionaires and billionaires 90 percent of their income. That sounds dubious to me, for others have told me that even if government confiscates 100 percent of the income of the rich, it would not come near to the amount required. And even if this policy were effective, would it even then be fair to put a 90 percent tax on some people's income?

In this case, I cannot just trust Sabrina as I could trust George. It isn't sufficient just to accept her perspective and add it to mine, as I did with George. Sabrina is not merely a set of sense organs that I could add to my own. Rather, she has done some thinking about reality from her own perspective, and she has added that thinking to what she considers her accumulated knowledge. But I cannot simply accept her testimony uncritically. I must make my own judgment.

So if I want to take up the question, I must do some research myself, or at least consult a greater number of authorities, in order to see if government can educate everybody by taxing the rich. But then I have to ask, what authorities are reliable? If Sabrina's ideas are not always reliable, where do I go to find the truth? I can read newspapers, books, and online material, but how do I judge, in each case, whether its testimony is reliable?

By my own intuition? In one sense, yes. Our judgments are our own. Again, we cannot step out of our own skin. But we all know that we, too, often make mistakes. If I judge that Sabrina's judgment is unreliable, I must admit that she may well have the same opinion of mine. Of course, both she and I must "use our own judgment." But that is tautological. That only means that we think what we think. It is not ground for claiming that the current contents of our minds are infallible, or even that they are better than someone else's. We often change our minds, deferring to someone who seems to have a better view than we have had up to now. We do not use our minds as static measuring sticks, rejecting every idea that disagrees with ours. At least we should not do this. We should be flexible enough so that occasionally we can learn something new, so that sometimes, at least, we can abandon old ideas and accept better ones, even better measuring sticks.

Knowing the world, then, is a complicated process in

constant change. It is a matter of interacting with our multitude of perspectives and with the perspectives of others, going here, then there.

But this sounds like we have no direction at all. We are like specks of dust, blowing in the wind, here and there, "tossed to and fro by the waves and carried about by every wind of doctrine" (Eph. 4:14). Is there no map telling us where to go? Is there no method for making the right choices?

ACCESS TO GOD'S PERSPECTIVE

The Bible teaches that God has granted us some access to his own perspective, the omniperspective, the perspective that includes and corrects all other perspectives. I say "some" access, not total access. Total access would mean that our mind is identical to God's, and that cannot be. God is the creator, and we are the creature. The discrepancy is not only quantitative, that God knows all the facts and we only know some. Rather, it is qualitative, that God's knowledge of every fact is different from our knowledge of the same fact. God knows, for example, that robins fly south in the winter; so do we. But God's knowledge of that fact is very different from ours, in many ways. For one thing, God's knowledge is original, ours derivative. God made the robins and equipped them to do what they do. The proposition, "robins fly south" is a proposition God has made to be true. When I say that robins fly south, I am stating something God has made to be true.

God's knowledge, therefore, is the *criterion* of ours. Our beliefs are true insofar as they measure up to God's. But God's are always true, just because they are his. He is his own criterion, the ultimate test of his own thoughts. But our thoughts do not serve as their own criterion. That is to say, they are not *autonomous*.

But, given the qualitative difference between God's thoughts and ours, God nevertheless enables us to gain some of his knowledge, to affirm the same truths he affirms. And when we do, we are incorporating, to some extent, God's perspective into our own.

REVELATION

Theologians use the term "revelation" to indicate the ways in which God enables us to incorporate his perspectives into ours. They distinguish:

(1) "General" or "natural" revelation, God revealing himself through the created world (Ps. 19:1; Rom. 1:18–21).

(2) "Special" revelation, God speaking human language to, and then through, prophets (Deut. 18:15–22), apostles (John 14:25), and the written text of Scripture (2 Tim. 3:15–17; 2 Peter 1:19–21).

(3) "Existential" revelation, God revealing himself through human beings as his "image" (Gen. 1:26–27). This includes his giving us ability to understand and apply other forms of revelation and therefore to develop our own sense of right and wrong (the "conscience," Rom. 2:15; 2 Cor. 4:2; 1 Tim. 1:5).[3]

In these ways, we gain *some* access to God's own perspective, as I described that access above. Much of the time, however, our knowledge of God's revelation is fragmentary and

---

3. I have discussed these various forms of revelation in *DWG* and in *ST*. "General" and "special" revelation are standard terms from the theological

uncertain. For example, we learn by natural revelation that the earth's climate has changed over the years. But the role of man's actions in recent climate change is debatable. We learn by natural revelation that food nourishes the body and also that some substances are toxic to human health. But just what is nourishing, and what is toxic, and in what quantities? These are subjects about which there is much disagreement. Over the years the consensus of human research has changed, and sometimes changed back again.

Even beliefs that some claim are based on the Bible are not always absolutely certain. Some people believe that Jesus expelled the money-changers from the temple at the beginning of his ministry (suggested by John 2:13–17). Others believe that he did this toward the end (suggested by Matt. 21:12–17). Many believe he did it twice, others that either Matthew or John reported this event out of chronological order. None of these views is immediately obvious or certain.

But there are some teachings of Scripture that are so clear and/or pervasive that nobody can question them. Scripture clearly teaches that there is one God, that Jesus is the eternal Son of God, that Jesus died for sinners and rose again, and that God promises salvation from sin to those who trust in Jesus' sacrifice and embrace him as Lord.

So God grants us certainty of the Bible's teaching, in many cases, by its sheer obviousness. But there is also a supernatural factor. Paul says to the congregation of a church he had planted, "Our gospel came to you not only in word, but also in power and in the Holy Spirit and with full conviction"

---

literature. "Existential" revelation is not, but is unique with me, so far as I know. I try to explain the reason for using a threefold, rather than merely twofold, division in these previous writings. Those who read the present book to its conclusion will also understand my preference for a threefold distinction.

(1 Thess. 1:5). That is, God sent his Holy Spirit to change the minds of these hearers, so that they would come to believe, and believe with assurance (see also 1 Thess. 2:13).

When that happens—that is, when God through our natural powers and the Spirit's supernatural influence convinces us that a certain belief is warranted by God's own speech—then God authorizes us to believe it with certainty, with assurance.[4] That means that there are certain propositions, such as "Christ died for sinners" that we can state on the authority of God himself. Like the prophets, we may preface these by saying "Thus says the Lord," or "This is what God says." In these cases, we can be certain that we have accessed God's own perspective on the truth, his omniperspective, which includes all other perspectives.

But, again, we do not have such certainty about everything. Humility and wisdom require us to distinguish when we have certainty and when we don't. And when we are uncertain, we should be eager to benefit from the perspectives of others—especially the omniperspective of God but also the limited perspectives of our fellow human beings made in God's image. The way to knowledge and certainty is the way of seeking additional perspectives, deeper perspectives.

PERSPECTIVES WITHIN PERSPECTIVES

We have seen that God's omniperspective is a complexity. It includes many perspectives within it. It includes the perspective of the fly on my office wall watching me type this manuscript, as well as all other possible and actual perspectives. There is something similar in our own thinking, which images that of God. In the image of God's omniperspectivalism, the

4. See my essay "Certainty," found as appendix A in HWPT, 582–88.

perspective of each human being incorporates perspectives from other human beings (like George and Sabrina) and from God. Even our knowledge of other perspectives is perspectival. When God considers the perspective of the fly on my office wall, he may well consider that perspective from my perspective, as I take notice of the fly and watch its progress from the top of the wall to the middle. I may consider Sabrina's politics, part of her perspective, from the perspective of, say, Charles Krauthammer, a political commentator. Or Krauthammer's perspective from Sabrina's. In human thought, as in God's, there are perspectives on perspectives on perspectives. Our thinking images God's even in its complexity.

This is one way in which God has made the world a unity. Everything can be understood from the perspective of everything else.

FOR REVIEW AND REFLECTION

1. Frame has mentioned perspectives relevant to the study of a tree. Suggest what perspectives might be relevant to the study of gravity. Of the history of Sweden. Of ethical methodology.
2. In one of these studies, show how some perspectives include others.
3. "People who use their reason to figure out the coherence of God's attributes . . . would be like my dog if he had tried to master the first sentence in my *ST*." Explain, evaluate.
4. How do you feel about God's omniperspectival knowledge? Is it a threat? A comfort? Hint: look at Psalm 139.
5. Have you ever gained knowledge that you considered intuitive? Describe how it differed from other knowledge.

6. Should we advise young people to "use your own judgment?" What qualifications should we put on that exhortation, if any?
7. Do we have access to God's perspective? How can we, given that his knowledge is omniperspectival? Discuss.
8. God's knowledge is the *criterion* of ours. Explain, evaluate.
9. "But there are some teachings of Scripture that are so clear and/or pervasive that nobody can question them." Explain, evaluate. If there are such teachings, give some examples.

GLOSSARY

autonomous. Thinking or acting without accepting any standard from outside ourselves.

criterion. A standard for judging the nature of something or the truth of a statement.

intuitive. Known by a process difficult to identify or describe.

omniperspectival. God's omniscience, understood as his ability to understand everything from every possible perspective.

omniscience. God's attribute of knowing everything.

perspective. A view of something by someone from somewhere.

pou sto. A place to stand (Archimedes). The starting point of an inquiry or endeavor, which gives insight and power.

qualitative difference. A difference in kind, not just quantity. One way to indicate the vastness of the difference between God's thoughts and our own.

revelation. Knowledge given by a source outside ourselves, particularly by God. See definitions in text of "general," "special," and "existential" revelation.

ring of truth. Our ability to judge the truth of a statement by way of our God-given intuition of what truth sounds like.

FOR FURTHER READING

John Frame, *DKG*. This was my first published book. It develops an epistemology (theory of knowledge) from the Bible and incorporates the concept of perspectives.

Vern S. Poythress, *Symphonic Theology: The Validity of Multiple Perspectives in Theology* (Grand Rapids: Zondervan, 1987). Poythress's first exposition of the idea of theology done from multiple perspectives.

PERSPECTIVES
AND THE TRINITY

GOD'S ATTRIBUTES AS PERSPECTIVES

We have seen that God has made a world full of perspectives in which everything is a perspective on everything else. That world, we have also seen, is a revelation of God. So we should understand that God, too, is a vastly complex being in which each of his attributes bears a perspectival relationship to all the rest.

God's attributes, the qualities by which Scripture describes God, are not "parts" of him. Rather, God is "simple," meaning that he has no parts.[1] He has no material parts because he is not a material being. And it is also wrong to think that his spiritual qualities, his attributes like love, wisdom, and power, are parts of him. When you remove a part of something (like a page from a book or a leg from a man) the whole may remain essentially the same. But if it were possible (and it is not) to separate God's wisdom from God himself, he would not be the God of the Bible.

---

1. On divine simplicity, see *DG*, 225–30; *ST*, 428–33.

Not only are God's attributes inseparable from him, but they are also inseparable from one another. His love is eternal; his mercy is just; his grace is all-powerful. The divine attributes all *have* divine attributes. In fact, each one has *all* the others. When we try to describe one attribute, we find that we are describing them all: his love, for example, is infinite, eternal, unchangeable. It is wise, just, good, true, all-powerful, all-knowing, omnipresent. So each attribute is a characterization of God as a whole and, therefore, of all the other attributes as well.

Since God's love is infinite, eternal, unchangeable, wise, just, and so on, God's love is God.[2] It can be nothing less than God since only God is infinite, eternal, and unchangeable. Similarly, God's wisdom is God; his justice is God; his power is God. I infer that each attribute presents a perspective on all the other attributes and on God's whole nature. We can learn about God from the perspective of his power, his justice, his grace, or any other attribute. And we can learn about one attribute from the perspective of any other.

One important implication is that God's attributes are personal qualities, not impersonal entities or forces. God's power, for example, is not an impersonal force but a person exerting his will. To "seek God's righteousness" is not to seek some physical law or metaphysical principle. It is not even to seek a part of God or a principle within God. It is to seek God

---

2. Scripture says that "God is love" (1 John 4:8) but not that "love is God." Preachers have often drawn attention to this difference. The problem with the latter expression is that we are apt to confuse God's love with human love so as virtually to worship the latter. God is not to be identified with finite love—certainly not with illicit love, which does exist. But divine love, the love that God himself gives, is different. God's love, the love that is his divine attribute, is nothing less than God himself. And the same may be said of his wisdom, goodness, grace, eternity, and so on.

himself. God's righteousness is God doing the right thing. God's power is God acting powerfully. God's love is God being kind to other persons.

Does this mean that all God's attributes are synonymous? I would hesitate to say that because synonymy is a property of words, and I am not sure that Bible translators and theologians have in every case (and in every language) come up with the most perfect vocabulary to describe the nature of God. But I do think it is right to think of the attributes as "perspectives." God's justice and his grace describe the same divine character but from different angles and different contexts. His justice is his whole being, understood from the perspective of legal rectitude. The same is true for his other attributes.

FATHER, SON, AND SPIRIT

The relations of God's attributes make clear that God is both one and complex. The nature of that oneness and complexity can be illumined by the idea of perspectives. But there is another way in which God is both one and many, and that has played a special role in the doctrinal confession of the church. That is the doctrine of the Trinity, the doctrine that God is one God (one substance, one essence, one being) in three persons (hypostases).

The Bible teaches clearly that God is one God (Deut. 6:4; 1 Cor. 8:4). But it ascribes divine attributes and actions to three that the church has called "persons": the Father, the Son, and the Holy Spirit. Each of these three is the one, true God.

Now it is tempting for me to say that these three persons are perspectives on one another, as I have said about God's attributes. But that would not be right. On that account, there would only be one divine person who can be described in three ways. But that is the ancient heresy of Sabellianism, or modalism, the view that the three persons are three "modes" or "forms" or "manifestations" of one person. That is not the view of Scripture. In the Bible, the three are distinct from one another. We see that in the fact that there are *transactions* between the three: the Father *sends* the Son (John 3:17); the Son *prays* to the Father (John 17); the Son *obeys* the Father (John 5:19); the Father and the Son *send* the Spirit into the world (John 14:26; 15:26); the Spirit speaks on the authority of the Father and Son, not on his own authority (John 16:13).

So the three are not interchangeable. Each has distinct tasks in the history of redemption. But even when carrying out those distinct tasks they are closely related to one another. The Father is "in" the Son, the Son "in" the Father, the Spirit "in" the Father and the Son.[3]

The three persons are all divine, equally worthy of worship. Each possesses the whole divine nature, and all the divine attributes. But they are different in some ways, as I have begun to indicate.[4] It is the Son, not the Father, who becomes incarnate and dies on the cross for our sins. It is the Father, not the Son, who authorizes the tasks that the Son and Spirit will perform in history (as John 5:19). It is the Spirit, not the Son or the Father, who changes the hearts of people to make them trust God (John 3). Yet as each performs his own task,

---

3. The traditional terms for this mutual indwelling are *circumincessio* and *perichoresis*.

4. The church has historically recognized the source of these differences in the "personal properties" of the three persons: The Father is unbegotten but begets the Son. The Son is begotten of the Father. The Spirit proceeds from the Father. The Western church, under the influence of Augustine, said that the Spirit proceeds from the Father "and the Son" (the famous *filioque*, rejected by the Eastern church). Begetting and proceeding are eternal events, so these events define the eternal distinct existence of each person.

he is "in" the other two, and the other two are "in" him. Each cooperates in every action of the others.

LORDSHIP ATTRIBUTES

I have found it helpful to generalize these biblical distinctions in the following ways:

1. The Father acts as *supreme authority* within the Trinity, establishing the eternal plan that the other persons bring into effect. In the world, the Father's plan demands all obedience.
2. The Son is the *executive power* of the Trinity, accomplishing what the Father ordains to take place. In the world, the Son's power accomplishes God's plan in all things.
3. The Spirit is the *pervasive presence* of the Trinity in all things. In the world, he applies God's plan to the depths of all reality and to the hearts of persons.

So, for example, in the Bible's doctrine of the Word of God, the Father is the speaker, the Son his powerful word, and the Spirit the "breath"[5] that conveys the word to its destination. So in Psalm 33:6 we read, "By the word of the LORD the heavens were made, and by the breath of his mouth all their host."

I call these descriptions of the three persons "lordship attributes." These describe the ways in which God rules the creation; that is, they describe God's *lordship*.

When Moses asked God's name, God replied by giving him the mysterious name *Yahweh*:

5. The Hebrew (*ruach*) and Greek (*pneuma*) words for "Spirit" also mean "wind" or "breath."

> Then Moses said to God, "If I come to the people of Israel and say to them, 'The God of your fathers has sent me to you,' and they ask me, 'What is his name?' what shall I say to them?" God said to Moses, "I AM WHO I AM." And he said, "Say this to the people of Israel, 'I AM has sent me to you.'" God also said to Moses, "Say this to the people of Israel, 'The Lord, the God of your fathers, the God of Abraham, the God of Isaac, and the God of Jacob, has sent me to you.' This is my name forever, and thus I am to be remembered throughout all generations. (Ex. 3:13–15).

The meaning of *Yahweh* is obscure, but as we can see, God relates it to the verb "to be" as employed in the phrases "I AM WHO I AM" and "I AM." English translators have typically rendered *Yahweh* as *Lord* (similarly with translations in other languages). So *Lord* has become the most common name of God in the Bible, used over 7,000 times. The name applies most often to God the Father but often also to Jesus Christ. There are also passages in which words attributed to Yahweh in the Old Testament are ascribed to the Holy Spirit in the New. Compare, for example, Jeremiah 31:33–34 with Hebrews 10:15–17.

When Scripture calls attention to the meaning of God's lordship, it typically focuses on three aspects that correspond to the three concepts defined above: lordship is God's *control*, *authority*, and *presence*. These are God's lordship attributes.

1. Yahweh is the *controller*, the one who invokes all the forces of nature to bring plagues on the Egyptians and deliver his own people (Ex. 3:19–20).
2. Yahweh is the supreme *authority* over human life, the one who always has the right to command and to be obeyed. He is the supreme *lawgiver* (Ex. 20:2–3; Lev. 18:4–5).

3. Yahweh is *present*, not only in the sense that he is omnipresent throughout the earth but in that he becomes intimately involved with a people. The culmination of the covenant between God and his people is Immanuel: God *with* us (Gen. 17:7; Rev. 21:3–4).[6] As he is the lawgiver, he is also the *grace-giver*.

These lordship attributes are perspectivally related:

1. God's *control* implies his authority and presence. Since God's control includes control over the world of obligation ("oughtness"), it entails his authority. And since it is comprehensive, it implies his presence; for how could God be omnipotent everywhere if he is not present everywhere?
2. God's *authority* implies his control and presence. He has the right to command everything he has made, which entails that he controls everything he has made. And his control and authority over every square inch of creation implies his presence in every square inch of creation.
3. God's *presence* implies his control and authority. For his presence is always the presence of the Lord. If he is present with any creature, then he has the ability to control and the right to command that creature.

Therefore, each of the lordship attributes includes the other two. They are not separate, but they are different ways of characterizing the complex unity that is God as he relates to his created world. Each, then, is a perspective on God, and each is a perspective on the other two.

---

6. For a full argument connecting the name Yahweh with these three lordship attributes, see my *DG*, 21–102.

You can see that in general the Father is associated with the lordship attribute of *authority*, the Son with *control*, and the Spirit with *presence*. But this distinction is not a sharp one. All three persons are the Lord, and they are related to the world as the Lord is related to his servants. This is an application of the *circumcessio*, the fact that each of the persons is "in" the other two. And it is an application of the perspectival relationship of the lordship attributes that I expounded in the previous paragraph.

SITUATIONAL, NORMATIVE, AND EXISTENTIAL

It is edifying to look at God, and his world, from the perspective of any one of his attributes. All the world reflects his justice (Ps. 89:14), his holiness (Isa. 6:3), his power (Ps. 65:6; 78:26), his wisdom (Ps. 104:24). As we saw, each divine attribute is God, seen from a particular perspective. So to recognize God's wisdom in the world is to recognize God himself. What a wonderful revelation, to know that God is present in all his creation, so that we can say, for example, that everything in our experience is made by the wisdom of God himself.

The same is true of God's *lordship* attributes. As we have seen, God's control, authority, and presence are manifest and effective everywhere, which is to say that God himself is in control, in authority, and present everywhere. All creation declares the glory of God (Ps. 19:1).

To study the course of nature and history is to study the course of God's *control* over his world. His control provides a perspective (I call it the *situational*) that sheds light on everything that happens. When the clouds glow with lightning and resound with thunder, that is the power of our God, his tool for controlling his world. When the fields abound with crops, that too is the power of God. When an earthquake sends tsunami waters to destroy houses and fields, that too is God's power. So we learn that God's power in nature is both grace and judgment. We learn from this the terror of God's wrath against sin and his power to make things right. So God's sovereign control characterizes our environment, our situation.

To study God's *authority* is to learn of the moral universe, the nature of obligation. That is to study the world from the *normative* perspective. Here we study the same world, the situation, but with a different emphasis. Here we learn of God as the lawgiver, the one who legislates our conduct, the one who rewards and punishes our behavior. Here we study the same universe as we studied from the situational perspective but with an emphasis of understanding our obligations. I call this the *normative* perspective.

We saw that everything in nature and history reveals God's control. But everything also reveals God's authority. In the garden of Eden, God charged Adam and Eve to replenish the earth and subdue it (Gen. 1:28). So Adam and Eve were to study every fact of God's world in order to determine how that fact could help them obey that command. When Adam found an almond tree, he saw that tree not only as a fact of God's universe but also as a way of carrying out God's command—to use it for food. Adam studied the world not only to identify God's facts but also to understand God's norms.

To study God's *presence* is to understand that all creation is his personal sanctuary (Isa. 66:1). This study covers the same facts as the situational and normative perspectives but, again, with a different emphasis. Here we observe that all the facts and events of nature and history are in fact manifestations of our personal God. Control and authority are not impersonal principles or forces. They are the thoughts and actions of the living God who has planned this narrative, who speaks through it, who judges the wicked, exalts the righteous, and communicates his love to all his people. This study of God's personal presence in everything is what I call the *existential* perspective.

We saw earlier that each genuine perspective includes the others, for every perspective deals with the same world. We saw how the lordship attributes include one another: his control includes his authority and presence and so on.

1. So the situational perspective includes the other two. Part of the situation is the moral universe and the omnipresence of God.
2. The normative perspective includes the other two. For God's norms require us to acknowledge his creation and interpretation of nature and history. They call us to believe in his control and in his omnipresence.
3. And the existential perspective includes the other two. For we discern God's personal presence precisely in his control over the world and over the moral universe.

Students sometimes ask me what perspective something is a part of: it seems like mountains are part of the situational perspective. Is that right? Well, yes. But they are also part of the normative, for they reveal God as lawgiver (Rom. 1:18–32).[7] Therefore, they are part of the existential as well, for they are a location of God's personal presence. So everything belongs to every perspective. And the three perspectives themselves belong to one another. So the normative perspective is part of our situation. The situation reveals God as the norm-giver. And the personal presence of God reveals to us both the nature of our situation and the content of our obligation.

7. God's anger makes the mountains tremble and quake (Ps. 18:7).

This is merely to say that perspectives are perspectives. They are not three *parts* of reality (any more than God's attributes are *parts* of him). Rather, each contains *all* reality, as an angle from which all reality can be understood. As God's might is part of his justice, so the situational perspective is part of the normative, and each perspective is part of the other two.

If I draw a circle to represent all of reality, the situational perspective is not a section of that circle, like a piece of pie. It is, rather, the whole circle, understood in a certain way. The same is true for the normative and existential perspectives.

But I prefer to diagram these relationships with a triangle rather than a circle:

Normative Perspective

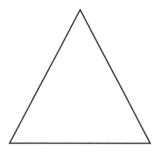

Situational Perspective   Existential Perspective

The whole triangle represents the contents of our experience and/or reflection. The corners are three angles from which we can look at that same subject matter. To study this reality from the normative perspective, we begin with the upper corner, asking what God has obligated us to do in our study. But to fully understand God's norms, we discover that we have to apply his commands to the situation before us (situational perspective) and to our own inner life (existential perspective). So we see how a full understanding of the normative perspective is not possible without an understanding of the other two perspectives.

Or we can begin with the question, what are the facts? That is to say, what is the situation? In this case, we look at the situational perspective. But we quickly learn that we cannot understand the situation without understanding our place in the situation (the existential perspective) and without understanding the norms governing the proper study of God's world (the normative perspective). So we cannot fully understand the situational perspective without the other two.

Or we may ask, how does all of this apply to me? That is to begin with the existential perspective. But we cannot understand who we are without understanding our environment (i.e., the situational perspective). And we cannot understand ourselves without understanding the obligations under which God has placed us (the normative perspective).

So the three perspectives are truly perspectives. None of them are *parts* of experience that we could study in isolation from the others. Rather, they are aspects of experience that incorporate and include one another. They are three *ways* by which we may interact with experience, three *emphases* of our study. But each includes the other two.[8]

FOR REVIEW AND REFLECTION

1. How is it that God (or anything else) can have no parts? Or is "simplicity" nonsense?

---

8. As we saw earlier, Vern Poythress defines "perspective" as "a view from somewhere. More precisely, it is a (1) view of something (2) by someone (3) from somewhere." This definition, as Poythress points out, is a triperspectival definition of "perspective." (1) is the "theme" (normative), (2) the person (existential), and (3) the context (situational). See Poythress, *Knowing and the Trinity: How Perspectives in Human Knowledge Imitate the Trinity*, 2018.

2. Each divine attribute *has* all the others. Give examples.

3. "God's attributes are personal qualities, not impersonal entities or forces." Explain. Why is this important?

4. Are the persons of the Trinity perspectives on one another? Why or why not?

5. Show how the distinctions between the persons of the Trinity entail the "lordship attributes."

6. Show how the three perspectives of human knowledge arise from the lordship attributes of God.

7. Show how each of the three perspectives includes the other two. Is anything limited to one perspective or another? Why or why not?

8. Describe the points of Frame's triangle.

GLOSSARY

attribute. A quality or predicate of something. The attributes of God are his perfections.

authority. The lordship attribute of God by which he has the right to be obeyed in everything he commands.

circumcessio. The doctrine that the Father, Son, and Holy Spirit are "in" one another. Synonymous with *Circumincessio*, *perichoresis*.

control. The lordship attribute of God indicating his power to determine all the events of nature and history.

existential perspective. A perspective of human knowledge, focusing on our internal subjective experience in close proximity to God's presence.

fact. A state of affairs, a component of the situational perspective.

filioque. Term added to the Nicene Creed in the Western church, indicating that the Holy Spirit proceeds from the Father *and the Son*, not from the Father only. *Filioque* means "and the Son."

lordship attributes. God's attributes of control, authority, and presence, which in Scripture define the nature of God's lordship.

normative perspective. A perspective of knowledge in which we focus on the world as a revelation of God's will.

personal. Able to know, think, plan, communicate verbally, etc.

personal properties. Qualities of the three Trinitarian persons that they do not share with one another. The Father has the property of eternally begetting the Son, the Son the property of being eternally begotten by the Father, and the Spirit the property of proceeding from the Father and the Son. (But see *filioque*.)

presence. The lordship attribute by which God is present to everything in the world.

Sabellianism. The heretical view that God is only one person who plays the roles of Father, Son, and Holy Spirit.

simplicity. God's quality of having no parts. His attributes are not parts of him but perspectives on his whole being; for example, God's love is God.

situational perspective. A perspective of knowledge in which we focus on the objects in the world.

Trinity. The Christian doctrine that there is one God in three persons, Father, Son, and Holy Spirit.

Yahweh. Divine name revealed to Moses in Exodus 3:15, generally translated *Lord* throughout Scripture.

FOR FURTHER READING

Augustine, *On the Trinity*. This is the definitive theological formulation of the Trinity in the Western church.

John Frame, *ST*. This book develops a triperspectival view of Scripture based on the doctrine of the Trinity. My actual exposition of that doctrine is at 421–515.

————, *DG*. This is my original discussion of God's nature and attributes. I develop the doctrine of the Trinity at 619–736.

Vern S. Poythress, *The Lordship of Christ: Serving Our Savior All the Time, in All of Life, with All of Our Heart* (Wheaton, IL: Crossway, 2016).

————, *Knowing and the Trinity: How Perspectives in Human Knowledge Imitate the Trinity* (Phillipsburg, NJ: P&R Publishing, 2018).

————, "Reforming Ontology and Logic in the Light of the Trinity," *Westminster Theological Journal* 57, 1 (1995), 187–219.

B. B. Warfield, "The Biblical Doctrine of the Trinity," in *The Works of Benjamin B. Warfield* (New York: Oxford University Press, 1927–32; Grand Rapids: Baker, 1991) 2:133–72. Citation refers to Oxford edition.

THE THREEFOLD GOSPEL

THE BIBLE TELLS us not only about God but about our-selves and our world. Indeed, its main purpose is to bring us some news about ourselves that we desperately need to hear. It is first bad news: we have sinned and fallen short of the glory of God (Rom. 3:23). Because of our sin, we deserve death as God's punishment (Gen. 2:17). But God is merciful beyond our imagination, and he has sent his Son Jesus Christ to die on the cross, to pay the penalty for our sin, so that we might have eternal life (see John 5:21–24; Rom. 6:23).

This salvation is the work of God the Holy Trinity. God the Father chose us in Christ before the foundation of the world (Eph. 1:3–4). The Son was born of the Virgin Mary and lived a human life, dying for our sins and rising again (Eph. 1:7–10). Then he and the Father sent the Spirit to regenerate, empower, and sanctify us (Eph. 1:11–14).

The gospel is the good news that tells us what God has done to save us. Triperspectivally, it tells us what God wants us to do (law), what God has done through the years to redeem us (history), and how God renews us from within by his Spirit (regeneration and sanctification). The Pentateuch or Torah, the first five books of the Bible, focuses on God's law, though that part of Scripture also contains history and stories of inner renewal. That part of Scripture emphasizes the normative perspective.

The books Joshua to Ezra and the four Gospels and Acts focus on narrating the history of redemption, the situational perspective.

The wisdom literature (Job–Ecclesiastes) and the letters of the New Testament teach readers particularly how to apply redemption to their hearts and to their life decisions.

The prophetic (Isaiah–Malachi) and apocalyptic (Revelation) books combine the perspectives, extending the readers' faith and hope into the indefinite future.

But the three perspectives are each found in all parts of Scripture. Consider the normative perspective. As I mention, the Mosaic law in the first five books of Scripture emphasizes the normative perspective. The Ten Commandments (Ex. 20:1–18; Deut. 5:6–22) set forth God's basic commands. But they clearly presuppose a situational context. In Exodus 19, God meets with Israel to establish a covenant with them. And existentially, they motivate our obedience, applying the law to our inward motives, as in the last commandment, "You shall not covet."

And God presents the law to us not only in the law of Moses but in all parts of the Bible. It is the book of Joshua that tells Israel to meditate on the law of God day and night (1:8). Indeed, since the whole Bible is God's word, it is all normative. Everything he says is to govern our lives and motivate our worship (2 Tim. 3:16–17).

Similarly, the situational perspective includes the whole Bible, for all of it is part of the Scripture's story of redemptive history. The Mosaic law comes to Israel as a great redemptive event, as does the coming of the Holy Spirit at the feast of Pentecost (Acts 2).

And the existential perspective exists on every page of

the Bible, for God intends every word of Scripture to be nourishment to our souls (Matt. 4:4). The law and the history are addressed to the heart of the reader.

So our rough and ready divisions of Scripture (law, history, wisdom, prophecy, etc.) do not sharply separate the three perspectives from one another. Because God is one God in three persons, his Word is a single triperspectival reality.

And as we have seen, each divine person exhibits the triperspectival lordship common to the whole Trinity. Of particular note, Jesus our lord and savior is the supreme prophet (authority), priest (presence), and king (controller).

LAW AND GOSPEL

Nevertheless, theologians and other Christians have been tempted to separate what God has brought together. Some traditional Protestant theology, mainly in the Lutheran tradition but also in the thinking of some Reformed writers, has maintained that God's law (our normative perspective) is completely separated from his gospel (understood as the narrative of redemptive events, the saving grace of God in history, our situational perspective).

This separation is an extrapolation from the biblical contrast between faith and works as means of salvation. Because our salvation is by faith alone, it is not at all by works (Eph. 2:8–10). So, on the separationist view, the message of law (by which we know what works are pleasing to God) should sharply be distinguished from the message of gospel (by which we know God's grace, what God has done for us through Christ). Because there is a sharp separation between grace and works, the argument goes, the message of grace must be sharply distinguished from the message of works (that is, the law). There is no grace or promise in the law, and there are no obligations in the gospel. The law arouses only terror, the gospel only joy and thanksgiving.

But this separation between law and gospel is not biblical.[1] The message of God's law is a redemptive blessing, a gift of God's grace: "Put false ways far from me and graciously teach me your law!" (Ps. 119:29). Further, the gospel message is a message about the triumph of God's law:

> How beautiful upon the mountains are the feet of him who brings good news, who publishes peace, who brings good news of happiness, who publishes salvation, who says to Zion, "Your God reigns." (Isa. 52:7)

The gospel is a message of cosmic renewal, the promise that the Great King will triumph over his enemies and establish his reign for all to see. And the gospel contains law: it tells people their obligation to repent and believe (Acts 2:38–39). And that obligation conveys God's promise to its hearers and their children (Acts 2:39). This promise brings joy to those who believe but terror to those who want to continue their rebellion against God. And when God proclaims the law, that proclamation is a delight to the righteous (Ps. 1:1–2) as much as it is a terror to the wicked.

Rather, we should see law and gospel as aspects of God's single message to the fallen human race. The law is his normative perspective, the gospel his situational perspective. It calls us to obey God and proclaims God's grace at the same time. It calls us to embrace a new way of life—trusting Jesus' sacrifice for our sins and obeying him as our lord.

---

1. I have argued extensively against the law/gospel distinction in my article "Law and Gospel," now available in Frame, *Selected Shorter Writings 3*, 186–98.

But doesn't the unity of the message break down the sharp biblical distinction between works and grace? Certainly not. We are saved by God's grace through faith alone, not of works, lest anyone should boast (Eph. 2:8–10). The one word of God tells us of our sin and at the same time of how God's saves sinners: "but God shows his love for us in that while we were still sinners, Christ died for us." (Rom. 5:8). We do not need two sharply different (and opposite) words to give us two different messages.

God's grace does not come by our works, but it demands our works as a response: "For we are his workmanship, created in Christ Jesus for good works, which God prepared beforehand, that we should walk in them" (Eph. 2:10). Our good works are a *response* to God's grace, a *result* of God's grace, not a price we pay for God's grace. For the very nature of grace is that there can be no payment for it. We can never *earn* God's grace or that salvation that comes from grace. But good works are the only appropriate response to God's grace, the only appropriate way to say thank you to God for his gift beyond measure.

OBJECTIVE AND SUBJECTIVE

Another way in which some people divide up the Word of God is by claiming that the real gospel is about objective realities, and that has nothing to do with our inner, subjective state. "Objective realities" are the events in history by which God accomplishes salvation: the incarnation, the cross, the resurrection. "Inner subjectivity" describes the transformation of human life as a result of these events. So inner subjectivity includes regeneration (the new birth) and sanctification (renewal of the heart and will).

Through church history, there have been movements that have focused on the inner life, such as medieval mysticism and Reformation-era quietism. One could argue that Protestant liberalism has often continued this emphasis. Neither the medieval nor the modern inwardness theologies have held orthodox biblical views of regeneration and sanctification. But there are many modern evangelicals who have spoken in more biblical terms about inner renewal.

Yet some who are more oriented toward confessional Protestant orthodoxy have disparaged evangelical emphasis on the inward life. They have said things like "the gospel is about what happens outside me, not what happens inside me."

As I disagreed with the law / gospel separation, I also disagree with the separation between outer and inner, between objective and subjective. The "objective" is aligned with what I have called the situational perspective (the facts of history), and the "subjective" is the existential perspective. But these cannot be separated. The situational perspective is a world that includes my inner life, and I understand objective facts by means of my inner ability to know. At the same time, the existential perspective is conditioned by its factual environment. My inner ability to know comes about through factors outside myself: my parents, my education, my experience, and especially God.

So when Peter preaches the gospel on the day of Pentecost, he promises that those who accept it will receive the "gift of the Holy Spirit" (Acts 2:38). The Spirit in Scripture renews our heart, our inner life. To learn Christ is to be changed in all aspects of our lives:

> To put off your old self, which belongs to your former manner of life and is corrupt through deceitful desires, and to be renewed in the spirit of your minds, and to put on the new self, created after the likeness of God in true righteousness and holiness. (Eph. 4:22–24)

The gospel is good news for the whole person, the subjective as well as the objective. It gives us the freedom to praise God, both for what he has done *for* us and what he has done (and continues to do) *in* us. In the gospel,

> God chose to make known how great among the Gentiles are the riches of the glory of this mystery, which is *Christ in you*, the hope of glory. (Col. 1:27, emphasis mine).

So in his revelation, in the preaching of the gospel, God discloses his law, the commands by which we are to live. He proclaims redemption, by which he saves us from our disobedience to his law. And he proclaims renewal of the heart, by which we live a new life of holiness and righteousness. None of these is separated from the other two. His law dictates the only terms by which we can be saved and renewed. Salvation fulfills the law by providing justice as well as love. Renewal enables the redeemed to fulfill the law (Rom. 8:4) and to be free from the law of sin and death (Rom. 8:1–2). In the gospel, God discloses his law, complete redemption, and the renewal we need to live the redeemed life.

SACRED AND SECULAR

Still others have tried to make a sharp distinction between God's word for the "sacred" sphere (the holy, the church, the worship of believers) and the "secular," "profane," or "common" sphere (culture, government, general knowledge).[2] These spheres are sometimes called God's "two kingdoms."

---

2. Some who have stressed this distinction in modern times have been Meredith Kline, Michael Horton, and David Van Drunen. I have critiqued these writers extensively in my *Escondido Theology*.

Certainly in Scripture there is a distinction between spheres that are more holy and those that are less holy. God is present everywhere, but he does set apart particular spaces in which his presence is especially intense. When Moses first met God in the bush that burned but was not consumed, God told him to remove his sandals, for the place was "holy ground" (Ex. 3:4–5). Other particularly holy places are Sinai the holy mountain, the tabernacle and temple (especially the inner court), the person of Christ (John 1:14), and the believer's body as the temple of the Spirit (1 Cor. 3:16–17).

And we should note that God's Word imposes special limits on those who enter sacred space. Moses had to remove his sandals near the burning bush, but in other places wearing them was acceptable.

But the two kingdoms theory seeks to expand this distinction to cover all areas of human life. Bringing incense to the temple, for example, is "holy" activity, while enforcing civil laws is "common" or "secular." In my view, Scripture does not make this distinction.

For one thing, the distinction in Scripture between holy and common is a relative distinction. The inner court of the temple is the holiest place in Israel. The outer court is also holy, but not as much, so that though it is relatively holy, it is also relatively common or profane. The entire temple is still less holy, as is the mountain (Zion) on which it rests. The whole people of Israel is God's holy people: holy in comparison to other nations, but less holy than the priesthood. And the ordinary Israelite believer is still less holy; but at least in the New Testament every believer is holy as the temple of the Spirit.

It is not as if there were a border fence through the world so that everything on one side is sacred and everything on the other side is secular. Indeed, in one sense the whole heaven and earth are holy as God's dwelling place:

> Thus says the LORD: "Heaven is my throne, and the earth
> is my footstool; what is the house that you would build for
> me, and what is the place of my rest? (Isa. 66:1)

Nor is there a line to be drawn through the various activities of human life so that some can be called sacred and others secular. For example, we usually think of worship as supremely "holy." But Paul says,

> I appeal to you therefore, brothers, by the mercies of God,
> to present your bodies as a living sacrifice, holy and accept-
> able to God, which is your spiritual worship. Do not be con-
> formed to this world, but be transformed by the renewal of
> your mind, that by testing you may discern what is the will of
> God, what is good and acceptable and perfect. (Rom. 12:1, 2)

In this context, worship is not attending a formal liturgy, but it is ethics: our attempt to obey God in all that we do and consequently to be different from the world. In this context, all of life is worship, and all of redeemed life is holy.

CONCLUSIONS

In this chapter I have been focusing on the gospel: God's good news announcing our salvation from sin. That gospel reflects God's Trinitarian nature: it is one and many. As many, it is triperspectival. It expresses God's law, the historical facts about Jesus, and the inner renewal that comes through the gift of the Holy Spirit.

Nevertheless, the gospel message is one as well as many. There is law in the gospel, gospel in the law. There is the objective in the subjective and subjective in the objective. And there is holiness in our common life and commonness in the holy.

FOR REVIEW AND REFLECTION

1. Describe the biblical gospel, showing how it is the work of God the Holy Trinity.
2. Outline the various sections of Scripture and show how each contributes to the gospel.
3. Describe the distinction between law and gospel (1) in Scripture and (2) in theological controversy.
4. Describe the distinction between objective and subjective and the theological controversy about it. Defend the true position as you see it.
5. Describe the "two kingdoms" controversy. Where do you think the truth lies? Why?

GLOSSARY

gospel. Good news, particularly the news that God has brought salvation to those who trust in Jesus.

grace. God's unmerited favor to those who deserve his wrath.

history. The series of events in time that is significant for human life and particularly for human salvation.

king. One appointed by God to rule over and subdue a nation to God's obedience. One of the "three offices" of Jesus.

law. The rules or norms that define obedience to God.

objective. Divinely established as fact, regardless of what creatures would prefer to believe.

priest. One appointed by God to bring sacrifice to him and to intercede for his people. One of the "three offices" of Jesus.

prophet. One appointed by God to set forth the word of God infallibly. One of the "three offices" of Jesus.

redemption. God's gracious acts to restore fallen human beings through the atonement of Christ.

regeneration. The new birth, in which the Holy Spirit creates in us a new heart of faith and obedience (John 3:3).

sacred. The sphere of God's holiness.

sanctification. The work of the Holy Spirit by which sinners are made holy.

secular. That which is not holy, but common or profane.

subjective. Existing in the human consciousness, mind, or feelings.

two kingdoms. The distinction between the sacred and the secular, according to some theologians.

works. Actions performed by persons, which in some cases are thought to merit reward.

FOR FURTHER READING

John Frame, *DKG*. See 319–46, on the place of subjectivity in theology.

———, *ET*. Essays on the two kingdoms theory and other issues.

———, "Law and Gospel," in Frame, *SSW3*, 186–98.

John Murray, *Redemption Accomplished and Applied* (Grand Rapids: Eerdmans, 1955). This is a carefully stated description of the various elements of salvation, including calling, regeneration, justification, adoption, and sanctification.

PERSPECTIVES
IN ALL OF LIFE

SO THE GOSPEL is good news for all of life. It establishes a relationship between us and Christ our lord, and as we have seen Christ's lordship can be understood triperspectivally. As the supreme prophet, priest, and king, he is the supreme authority, presence, and controller. In these respects, he reflects the lordship attributes of the whole Trinity.

These offices of Christ are especially precious to us when we think about salvation itself. But as we have seen, his salvation transforms all of human life. He is prophet, priest, and king in all areas of life. When believers go to the workplace, they bring their faith with them: "So, whether you eat or drink, or whatever you do, do all to the glory of God" (1 Cor. 10:31). And when they do that, their workplace will never be the same. So the gospel changes all of life. For it creates new people, as new creations of God (2 Cor. 5:17).

New historical realities emerge. Renewed people bring about advances in worship and liturgy but also in business, the arts, government, entertainment, care for the sick and the poor, and all the academic disciplines. As for the academic disciplines in particular, my colleague Vern Poythress has published a series of books about "redeeming" different spheres of human life, such as science,[1] sociology,[2] mathematics,[3] and philosophy.[4] The point of these titles is not that redemption extends to these disciplines in just the same way it extends to individual believers. Rather, redeemed people take their faith to the academy and find in God's revelation new and cogent ways of understanding his creation. This new understanding can lead to beneficial cultural change.[5]

As Poythress indicates, when we bring our faith to the workplace and the academy, it is important for us to learn how to see the creation as God's Word presents it, not as we in our sinful autonomy would like it to be. The Bible is not a textbook of science, or mathematics, or politics, but what it says about these disciplines is true because it is God's word. And whatever we discover as Christian laborers and academics will necessarily agree with what the Bible says. I am not saying that there is a distinctively biblical way to hammer a nail. But when we hammer nails into wood, we should do it to advance projects that will bring glory to God.

That new biblical understanding of things will have a triperspectival aspect to it because the whole creation is the work of our Triune God. Everything reveals God's norms, the facts he has created, and the inner life of the person who

1. Poythress, *Redeeming Science: A God-Centered Approach* (Wheaton, IL: Crossway, 2006).

2. Poythress, *Redeeming Sociology: A God-Centered Approach* (Wheaton, IL: Crossway, 2011).

3. Poythress, *Redeeming Mathematics: A God-Centered Approach* (Wheaton, IL: Crossway, 2015).

4. Poythress, *Redeeming Philosophy.*

5. Poythress summarizes well the principle of recognizing Christ's lordship in all areas of life in his *The Lordship of Christ: Serving Our Savior All of the Time, in All of Life, with All of Our Heart* (Wheaton, IL: Crossway, 2016).

seeks to understand. But as we shall see, these three objects of knowledge are not rigidly separated. There are norms in the facts; the norms are themselves facts; and the norms and facts are elements of our subjective experience.

In this chapter I shall explore how a triperspectival understanding can help us respond to all aspects of the world God has made. There are three main types of response we make to the revelation of God in the world: knowing, choosing, and feeling. I will look at each of these and try to understand how each relates to the others and how each illumines aspects of our knowledge and life.

KNOWING[6]

We tend to think of knowledge as fundamental to all human activity in God's world. To grow corn, we need to know what corn is, how it grows, and many other facts. So it seems that human activities begin with knowledge. Of course, knowledge is not only a beginning. Early knowledge leads to later knowledge. And much knowledge comes to us in the course of other activities. Very rarely, if ever, do we engage in knowing without at the same time doing something else. So as knowledge assists us in our other activities, the reverse is also true.

For knowledge to exist, there must be facts (the subject matter we seek to know), minds able to know those facts, and norms or rules for determining when the mind has correctly identified and interpreted the facts. In our triperspectival understanding, the facts represent the situational perspective, the mind the existential perspective, and the norms the normative perspective.

6. I have discussed knowledge far more extensively in *DKG* and in *ST*, 695–767.

These three factors in knowledge might seem to be sharply distinguishable. In fact, some may think it important to distinguish them sharply from one another. For example, it would seem wrong to identify the human mind with its factual objects of knowledge. That would confuse the object with the subject and would suggest that reality is whatever the mind wants it to be. But recall that in the last chapter I indicated reasons why we should not draw, in our theology, a sharp distinction between the objective and the subjective. The subject, the mind, is itself an object of knowledge, and the objects of knowledge are those that the mind identifies as such.

So I maintain that the three elements of knowledge are perspectivally related. Each embraces the other two. (1) The facts (situational) include the norms and the mind: minds and norms are among the factual objects about which we seek knowledge. (2) The mind (existential) includes the facts and the norms, for we know facts and norms only through our minds. The facts and norms are what the mind acknowledges to be facts and norms. And (3) the norms (normative) define what the facts are and the proper workings of the mind in identifying them. For various purposes, we may want to focus on one or two of these. But it is never possible to divide any of them sharply from the other two. To answer questions about the facts, we need answers about the norms and the mind, and so on.

Facts, norms, and mind: the relations of these govern the study of knowing (epistemology). And the history of epistemology has been a history of theories on the relationships of these factors.[7] For Plato, for example, the world of forms (normative) defines the world of sense experience (situational).

7. I have discussed the history of epistemology at length (together with other philosophical and theological issues) in my *HWPT*. See especially the

The objects of sense experience perplex us, but the forms tell us what they really are. But the two worlds are different and contrary to one another (e.g., the forms are perfect and the world of sense imperfect), so the forms are unable to do their job—namely, to define the objects of the world of sense. Plato thinks that the human mind (existential) is able to bridge this gap, but that thesis leaves unclear how the mind is related to the other two categories.

The problem is autonomy. Plato does not acknowledge the God of the Bible. For him, the forms, sense objects, and human minds are "just there," autonomous and independent. God plays no role in creating, redeeming, or coordinating these, so there is no reason for us to expect them to be coordinated.

In the rationalist tradition (Descartes, Spinoza, Leibniz), human reason has the final say as to what is truth. It is the normative and therefore the final truth. But what ground is there for thinking that human reason is reliable enough to serve as the final criterion of truth and knowledge?

The empiricist tradition (Locke, Berkeley, Hume), opposing the rationalists, believes that sense experience (the situational perspective) is the ultimate standard of truth. But they had to admit that sense experience does not reveal ultimates, that it does not warrant certainty. How, then, can it be an "ultimate" standard of anything?

So as with Plato the conversation eventually appeals to the autonomous human mind (existential) to make the final judgment, a judgment appropriate only for God to make.

In a theistic epistemology, God creates the facts of the world so that they can be understood only by his norms. He reveals the norms by his Word, his revelation. And he makes

---

introductory chapter, "Philosophy and the Bible," 1–45.

human beings so that they can understand the facts of creation according to the norms he has revealed.

CHOOSING

One popular way of understanding the human mind is to say that it consists of intellect, will, and emotions. The intellect is associated with "knowing," the will with "choosing," and the emotions with "feeling." Plato believed that the intellect should rule human life and that conviction has also appeared from time to time among Christian thinkers.[8] Others (like Duns Scotus and Soren Kierkegaard) have endorsed the primacy of will, and still others (like David Hume, Jean-Jacques Rousseau, and Friedrich Schleiermacher) have believed that feeling is and should be the main influence in human life.

The activity of choosing, however, is similar in many ways to the activity of knowing. The inquiries that lead to knowledge are a series of choices. If I seek to know something about plate tectonics, for example, I choose to study books on the subject, gather equipment to make precise observations, and construct experiments on it. Each choice leads to greater knowledge, and greater knowledge in turn leads to more significant choices. Knowledge refines my choices, and my choices refine my knowledge—a virtuous circle, when the project is going well.

Like knowing, choosing is a triperspectival process. To make the best choices, I must understand the situation before me, follow the best rules for decision making, and satisfy myself that I have done these things right. Situational, normative, existential.

---

8. J. Gresham Machen and Gordon H. Clark are two examples. Both spoke of the "primacy of the intellect."

In that way, we can also understand choosing as a species of knowledge, and vice versa. To know a fact, I must choose the right methods and procedures, and once I have made those choices, I have the knowledge I sought. And when I seek knowledge in that way, I have made the choices that are best for me.

Knowing and choosing are different perspectives on obedience to God. Responding properly to God's revelation can be described either as knowledge or as choosing: a knowledge based on choice or a choice based on knowledge.

FEELING

I suggested that knowing and choosing are essentially the same: mutually dependent, alternate descriptions of our responses to God's revelation. Feeling, or emotion, I believe, may be added as a third way of understanding our responses to God.

Many thinkers regard feeling, or emotion, as the most extreme opposite of the working of the intellect. The intellect says "I know," "I think," or "I believe," while the emotions say "I feel." But what is the precise difference between a feeling and a conviction? Both are based on data from introspection. A belief is a fact about my inner experience; a feeling is that as well. Thought is an attempt to put feelings into words.

I do not understand why "I believe it is hot" cannot be a working synonym for "I feel it is hot." When someone tells me that "General Pershing fought in World War I" and I agree with that assertion, I say "I believe that." But why shouldn't I say that my belief is a feeling that I have toward that assertion?

In the previous chapter I objected to the notion that the gospel is wholly objective and not at all subjective. Here I am generalizing the point I made earlier. Every statement of an objective truth is a subjective response to data presented to me.[9]

CONCLUSION

Knowing, choosing, feeling: three responses to the world in which God has placed us. They are perspectivally related. To know is to make appropriate choices and to respond appropriately to data. To choose is to act by following appropriate feelings about knowledge. To feel is to experience appropriately the data presented by my choices and knowledge. All three of these responses to the world are triperspectival.

FOR REVIEW AND REFLECTION

1. Define the three offices of Christ. How do these reflect the lordship attributes of the Trinity?
2. Is it legitimate to talk about "redeeming" science and sociology, or only about redeeming sinful human beings? Defend your answer.
3. Distinguish between facts, mind, and norms as aspects of human knowledge. Are these perspectivally related? Why or why not?
4. Describe the philosophical controversy over the relation between forms and sense experience. Do you see any promising solutions for these issues?
5. Do you believe in the "primacy of the intellect?" Define the phrase and defend your answer. How are knowing, choosing, and feeling related to one another?

---

9. For more reflection on the relation between convictions and feelings, see chapter 7.

GLOSSARY

emotion, or **feeling**. That aspect of the human mind associated with self-awareness.

empiricism. The philosophical theory that human sense experience is the ultimate source of truth.

epistemology. The study of knowledge.

forms. The qualities that make everything what it is. In Plato's philosophy, forms exist in a realm distinct from the world of our experience.

intellect. That aspect of the mind associated with knowing.

knowledge. Ability to act appropriately in regard to facts, norms, and / or the inner life.

primacy of the intellect. The theory that truth comes first into the intellect and thereafter to the will and emotions. The theory often asserts that the intellect should be more central than the will and emotions to human decision making.

rationalism. The philosophical view that human reason is the ultimate source of knowledge.

will. That aspect of the mind associated with choosing.

FOR FURTHER READING

John Frame, *DKG*. My study of human knowing, based on Scripture.

———, *HWPT*. Contains discussions of the philosophical movements and ideas discussed in this chapter.

———, *ST*, 695–767. A summary and revision of the discussion of epistemology in *DKG*.

Vern S. Poythress, *The Lordship of Christ: Serving Our Savior All of the Time, in All of Life, and with All of Our Heart* (Wheaton, IL: Crossway, 2016).

———, *Redeeming Mathematics: A God-Centered Approach* (Wheaton, IL: Crossway, 2015).

———, *Redeeming Philosophy: A God-Centered Approach* (Wheaton, IL: Crossway, 2016).

———, *Redeeming Science: A God-Centered Approach* (Wheaton, IL: Crossway, 2006).

———, *Redeeming Sociology: A God-Centered Approach* (Wheaton, IL: Crossway, 2011).

THE NORMATIVE
PERSPECTIVE

FACTS AND NORMS

In the next three chapters, I will discuss some issues that arise with the three individual perspectives as we seek to use them to the glory of God. Under the normative perspective, I shall consider first the basic difference between norms and facts, between the normative and the situational.

The distinction between normative and situational perspectives corresponds with the common distinction between facts and norms. Facts constitute what *is* the case, and norms constitute what *ought* to be the case. Often we state facts in the indicative mood (e.g., "We took that course last semester") and norms in the imperative (e.g., "Wipe your feet on the mat outside"). But it is also possible to express norms in the indicative, with words like "should," "ought," and "must" (e.g., "You really should wipe your feet on the mat outside").

Norms are our obligations, and facts are the world in which we must carry out those obligations. In some contexts, we need to be reminded that norms and facts are different. For example, the philosopher G. E. Moore discussed what he called the "naturalistic fallacy," which is an illegitimate attempt to deduce a norm from a fact. An example would be "Airbags prevent deaths in car accidents; therefore, the government should require airbags in all cars." This quote could be the outline of a persuasive political argument, but it is not a valid argument as it stands. There may be a better way of dealing with the problem than government action. "Airbags prevent deaths" is a statement of fact; "government should require airbags" is the statement of a norm. So many have argued that we should never reason from facts to norms.

But facts and norms are very closely related. If "airbags prevent deaths" is a fact, then it is a fact we *ought* to acknowledge and act on. We could even define fact that way: a fact is a situation we ought to acknowledge and act on. And we could also define norm in terms of fact: a norm is an obligation that we should recognize as fact.

The problem with the naturalistic fallacy is not that it reasons from fact to norm but that it fails to justify its normative conclusions. In the argument above, we could repair the difficulty by formulating it this way:

1. Airbags prevent deaths.
2. Government is obligated to require anything that prevents deaths.
3. Therefore, government is obligated to require airbags.

Premise #2 is controversial, of course. But if it is true, then the whole argument is valid. So with #2 as a mediating premise, the argument may legitimately proceed from fact (#1) to norm (#3).

So the following is not a naturalistic fallacy:

1. God has said, "Do not covet."
2. Therefore, we are obligated not to covet.

God's speaking is a fact, and it immediately entails obligations. That, at least, is the teaching of Scripture.[1]

This discussion is a defense of the point I made in chapter 2 and later—namely, that the normative perspective and the situational perspective are ultimately identical. They are perspectives on the world, and therefore perspectives on one another. It would not be wrong to define "fact" as a situation we *ought* to acknowledge, or to define "norm" as a fact that governs our behavior. Norms and facts are perspectively related.[2] They are different, but the difference is a difference between two perspectives.

NORMS AND REVELATION

How does God reveal our obligations? In all of reality. That is what I mean by saying that the normative perspective is a perspective on everything.

Return to our discussion of revelation in chapter 1. It is evident that God reveals himself in everything because nothing can be what it is without him. So in "natural revelation," everything reveals God (Ps. 19:1; Rom. 1:18–21). Natural revelation

---

1. It is a naturalistic fallacy if one tries to use such arguments apart from the biblical worldview. Non-biblical thought has no basis for determining obligation, so it cannot justify a logical move from a fact to an obligation. In our example, if God doesn't exist, there is no reason to think that government is obligated to prevent deaths—or that it is not so obligated. But if God does exist, then he exists as the world's chief norm as well as the world's chief fact, so what he says is law for us.

2. And both of these are perspectively related to the third category on our triangle: personal experience. I shall discuss that point in chapter 7.

includes ethical content; it reveals human obligation. According to Romans 1, God not only reveals in the natural world the fact that he exists (verses 19–20), but he also reveals how people should respond to these facts. Once you know that God exists, you should "honor" him (verse 21). To honor him means to worship him alone (not idols, verse 23) and to obey his laws for our behavior (verses 24–32). So revelation is not only a revelation of facts but also a revelation of norms.

So everything we see, hear, touch, or taste dictates how we should behave. In 1 Corinthians 10:31, Paul tells us that whether we eat or drink or whatever we do, we should do all to the glory of God. So when we see an apple, for example, we should ask how we should use this fruit to the glory of God. Every apple, every tree, every stone, every person reveals norms for our lives.

Of course, to apply 1 Corinthians 10:31 this way is to bring together natural and special revelation. Scripture is a sufficient set of norms for our lives (2 Tim. 3:15–17), and God wants us to see all of natural revelation in the light of the biblical standard. Everything the Bible says is normative for us. In that respect, Scripture is *law*.

And, as I discussed in chapter 3, it is also *gospel*, the good news about Jesus. People sometimes say that the gospel has no law in it because they want to draw a sharp distinction between law and grace. But the gospel does have commands embedded in it: commandments to repent and believe. Keeping these commandments is our normative obligation.

To say that the gospel entails obligations is not to say that we are saved by works. We are saved entirely by what God does, not by what we do. We do not earn salvation by what we do; it is a free gift. But we are obligated to respond to God's grace by obeying him.

So the normative perspective includes everything that

God has made and everything that God has said to us. That is, it includes everything. God calls us to walk through his creation, looking at everything and determining our obligation in every situation. Just as he commanded Adam to determine how to have dominion over every situation to the glory of God, so he wants us to respond to every fact in our experience to the glory of God. To do that is to know the world from the normative perspective.

FOR REVIEW AND REFLECTION

1. What is "the naturalistic fallacy?" Give an example of it.
2. Is it a naturalistic fallacy to say "God has commanded x, therefore I must do x?" Why or why not?
3. Is it possible to derive God's norms from natural revelation? Explain.

GLOSSARY

facts. What are the case. States of affairs.

naturalistic fallacy. G. E. Moore's term for arguments that begin with factual (non-normative) premises and seek to derive normative conclusions. Reasoning from "is" to "ought." An argument that fails to justify its normative conclusions.

norms. What God requires of us. Obligations. What *ought* to be the case.

FOR FURTHER READING

John Frame, *DKG*.

———, *DCL*. In this book I deal with the three perspectives as a Christian system of ethics. In ethics, of course, the "ought," and therefore the normative perspective, plays a particularly important role. I discuss here in many contexts the relation of norms to facts and feelings.

Vern S. Poythress, *Redeeming Science* and the other "Redeeming" books noted in previous chapters. In all these disciplines, the three perspectives play their roles.

Cornelius Van Til, *Christian Theistic Ethics*. Available at https://presupp101.files.wordpress.com/2011/08/van-til-christian-theistic-ethics.pdf.

————, *A Christian Theory of Knowledge* (Nutley, NJ: Presbyterian and Reformed, 1969).

————, *A Survey of Christian Epistemology* (Philadelphia: Den Dulk Christian Foundation, 1969). Considers the theory of knowledge historically, including a thorough critique of Plato.

THE SITUATIONAL
PERSPECTIVE

THE "FACTS" PLAY a special role to modern people. We have often heard accounts of the history of thought that go somewhat like this: Ancient and medieval people explored the world by way of tradition and mythology, but modern man has made a great advancement beyond such primitive methods. We moderns have learned to seek *facts*. The movement of philosophical empiricism, connected with names like Locke, Berkeley, and Hume, thought that much philosophy, even in its own day, was not a true search for facts but a spinning out of theories backed only by speculation.[1] The empiricists sought a philosophy based not on tradition, or even on logic in itself, but on *observation* and *experiment*. It is by these, they thought, that we discover what truly is, what are the facts.

Advocates of science picked up the empiricist theme: only an observational method will tell us what the facts really

1. The target of this criticism was often the rationalistic systems of Descartes, Spinoza, Leibniz, and others.

are. (But is such a method capable of accessing invisible realities?) And journalists have often drawn a sharp line between fact and opinion, insisting that the latter be fully justified by the former.

So in Christian thought, recent centuries have focused more than before on facts of history, on archaeology, on linguistics, on the pronouncements of scientists as to what is possible. Apologists have focused on *evidence* rather than rational proofs, as Thomas Aquinas did.

But along with this emphasis on fact, many have paid less attention to what I have called the normative perspective, as focused in the authority of Scripture. Apologists have sometimes argued that we should not appeal to Scripture, since Scripture is precisely what is in question. If we appeal to Scripture to prove the truth of Scripture, we would be engaging in circular argument. So it is better, the argument goes, to argue the truth of Christianity from fact alone (meaning extrabiblical facts), and from those facts to derive conclusions about the truth of Scripture.

But there are fatal confusions in this line of reasoning. First, what do we mean by "fact"? If God exists, shouldn't we say that the existence of God is a fact? If the Bible is God's word and therefore inerrant, then isn't its inerrancy a fact? The fact-centered apologetic we have been considering is somewhat confused about what the facts are and which ones we should consider as evidences for Christianity. Apologists often seem to think that biblical teachings should not be considered facts, but something else. But that is not cogent. Biblical teachings, like "God is three in one," if they are true (as Christians believe they are) have to be regarded as facts.

If this is true, then biblical norms are factual, and these biblical facts govern our ideas about other facts. And since facts are to be believed, they are norms. True facts are normative, and authoritative norms are factual. That suggests that there is no ultimate difference between norms and facts, but they are best distinguished according to a perspectival model.

To talk about norms is to view the whole world as a revelation of God. To talk about facts is to view the whole world as God's creation, the world as he has made it to be. Norms impose on us God's lordship attribute of authority. Facts impose on our minds the actual world as God has made it to be, through his creation and providence—God's lordship attributes of power and control. But of course the facts also display God's authority, for the facts are what God has ordained the world to be. And the norms display God's creative power, for they tell us how we should think about what God has made.

So the two are related perspectivally. Norms and facts are two different ways of describing the world God has made. We cannot understand the facts until we listen to what God has said about them (i.e., the norms). And we cannot understand the norms until we see the facts—that is, until we see how those norms apply to the world God has made. Instead of facts competing with norms, we encounter a situational perspective that is identical with the normative perspective, though with a different emphasis.

How does this understanding affect our apologetics? It is still perfectly legitimate to present facts so that people will believe. This is what Paul does in 1 Corinthians 15:1–11 as he lists witnesses of the resurrection of Jesus Christ. But he lists these evidences in the context of God's revelation. He is not presenting "brute facts" or "bare facts." Indeed, his clinching argument is that these facts are warranted by the normative Word of God, the revelation Paul brought to Corinth in his original preaching of the gospel (see verses 1–3, 11–12, 14–15). Yes, indeed: present the facts. But present them consistently with God's revelation.

Laws and facts, norms and situations, describe one world—God's world—from two perspectives. I call them the normative and the situational perspectives. But there is still another way to look at God's world.

FOR REVIEW AND REFLECTION

1. Show the relation of the situational perspective to the scientific method. Is the latter limited to the former?
2. "If we appeal to Scripture to prove the truth of Scripture, we would be engaging in circular argument." Explain, reply.
3. "There is no ultimate difference between norms and facts, but they are best distinguished according to a perspectival model." Explain, evaluate.
4. Does Paul defend the resurrection of Christ by a factual apologetic in 1 Corinthians 15? If so, how does he qualify that factual apologetic?

GLOSSARY

empiricism. The view that human sense experience is the ultimate criterion of knowledge and truth.

evidence. Alleged facts adduced to prove or verify a conclusion.

facts. States of affairs, objects of knowledge. "Brute facts" or "bare facts." Facts thought to be separate from any interpretative activity.

FOR FURTHER READING

John Frame, *DKG*. Discusses at length the place of facts and the situational perspective in human knowledge and apologetics.

————, *HWTP*. Discusses various positions on epistemology, including rationalism and empiricism.

Vern S. Poythress, *Redeeming Philosophy* and *Redeeming Science* discuss the role of perspectives in factual knowledge.

THE EXISTENTIAL
PERSPECTIVE

THERE IS SOMETHING remarkable about knowledge of the self, which led Socrates to admonish his students, first of all, to "know yourself." To know anything, you need to understand that you yourself are part of the story. Your knowledge begins with feelings within your body. It grows as a perspective that begins with your body and extends to a perceptual field that is vast. When you look at the sky or the ocean, that perceptual field is virtually infinite; you cannot count the things you see. When you consider the reality of God's presence in the world, the reach of your mind is actually infinite, for you are peering into the very nature of God.

But even though your perspective may reach to infinity, there is a sense in which it remains within you. When you perceive the world, you are perceiving your own visual field. When you hear sounds, you are hearing your own aural field. So in an important sense, all knowledge is self-knowledge. That does not imply the skeptical ("solipsistic") conclusion that you cannot know anything outside yourself. But it does imply that all of your knowledge is mediated by knowledge of yourself.

And so self-knowledge influences all other knowledge. You are a knower—with powers of sensation and reason and with powerful motivations to understand the world around you. So another great Greek philosopher, Aristotle, explaining why he wrote a book on metaphysics, said "All men by nature desire to know." You need to understand not just your powers of knowledge but why you seek knowledge, the human goals that you seek to attain by knowing the world. And you need to understand the barriers to knowledge within yourself: the weaknesses of your senses and reason, and the biases that often lead you to false conclusions.

As we have seen, the Bible tells us that God's revelation of himself is perfectly clear; every human being knows him at one level, but we "suppress" the truth (Rom. 1:18) because we would rather believe a lie (verse 25). So when we seek to know anything, we must make special efforts to know ourselves and to restrain in ourselves those tendencies that suppress the truth rather than affirm it.

So we cannot know other things rightly unless we know ourselves.[1] All our means of knowledge are found in our own faculties: our sight, our hearing, our touch, our taste, our reasoning, our faith, our presuppositions. So if we were able to know ourselves as Socrates urges, we would know everything else that we are capable of knowing.

On the other hand, the reverse is also true. We come to know ourselves by knowing the world outside us. We cannot know ourselves unless we know our environment (the situational perspective) and unless we understand the principles and rules governing our attempts to know (the normative perspective). So knowing yourself and knowing the world

---

1. Recall Calvin's assertion on the first page of the *Institutes* that we cannot know ourselves rightly unless we know God, and *vice versa*.

outside yourself are the same thing, viewed from two perspectives.

I call the focus on self the *existential perspective*. As we have seen, the existential perspective includes the other two. But the other two perspectives can be accurately understood only from their relation to the self, so they presuppose and include the existential perspective. The same holds for all the perspectives we have discussed: each perspective includes the other two.

I mentioned that the existential perspective includes the deliverances of our senses and reason and therefore includes everything in the world. But senses and reason are only part of self-knowledge. When we look carefully and reflect on our own nature as God has created it, we respond in awe:

> I praise you, for I am fearfully and wonderfully made. Wonderful are your works; my soul knows it very well. (Ps. 139:14)

> What is man that you are mindful of him, and the son of man that you care for him? Yet you have made him a little lower than the heavenly beings and crowned him with glory and honor. You have given him dominion over the works of your hands; you have put all things under his feet, all sheep and oxen, and also the beasts of the field, the birds of the heavens, and the fish of the sea, whatever passes along the paths of the seas. O LORD, our Lord, how majestic is your name in all the earth! (Ps. 8:4–9)

Consider your dreams, your imagination, your intuition, your feelings, your artistic sensitivities. Consider the commitments that serve as presuppositions to your quest for knowledge. Within us there are capacities that have not been much studied but which access untold depths of God's creation. There may well be uncharted senses or ESP. "Human subjectivity" describes a dimension without precise shape, but it is of vast importance to us as we seek to know God's world.

Often we find ourselves knowing something but unable to say clearly how we know it. Perhaps we will credit such knowledge to "intuition." Or it may come from a synergistic confluence of many capacities. In such situations, we are tempted to say "I feel that it is true." Intellectualists are rarely happy with such testimonies. They don't want to hear about what we feel, only about what we think. But, as I argued in chapter 4, the difference is actually not a sharp one. Sometimes our senses, reasons, and intuitions reinforce one another, and we find that they have left us with a conviction. We cannot always track this process precisely. I cannot doubt that often the best way to express this knowledge is by "I feel this is so."

But even in this most "subjective" kind of knowledge, the existential perspective presupposes the other two. The depth of our subjectivity is also a depth in our moral sense (the normative) and in our perception of our environment (the situational). So the existential perspective reveals to us some of the depth in the other two perspectives.

That depth enters every inquiry. When I seek knowledge of, say, Alexander Hamilton, much of my research is focused on the situational (Hamilton's biography) and normative (the values that governed Hamilton's decisions) perspectives. But often I struggle between two opinions. Was Hamilton a Christian or a deist? Some facts point in one direction, others in another. Some of his values point one way, some otherwise. Where should I come down on the question? On Monday I am persuaded that he was a deist because of some evidence. On Tuesday, I am persuaded that he was a Christian, looking at different evidence. Back and forth I go, reviewing the evidence.

Of course, the quest may be fruitless; I may never be able to gain certainty. But sometimes conviction appears. It may seem to come out of nothing. It is not necessarily that a new piece of evidence appears or that I interpret an old piece differently. But the whole shape of the evidence changes in my mind. So on Wednesday I find myself convinced of one conclusion or another. The process can be quite mysterious.

I sometimes call this phenomenon "cognitive rest." It is like finishing a task. I have been sifting through evidence and arguments and sources. Suddenly it jells, and I don't feel the need to do any more research on the subject. Now I can say "I know." The coming of certainty is like a feeling. Indeed, feeling is perhaps the best way to describe it.

So in one sense the process of knowing reduces to feeling—the sense that all my work has jelled into a meaningful shape. That jell is what gives me cogent understanding of all the facts, the arguments, the principles.

But when people ask me about the source of that certainty, I usually don't speak vaguely of a jell, or a cognitive rest, or a feeling. I rather present arguments based on senses and rational inference. But I know I would not have seen the evidence this way except through the feeling of cognitive rest. The rest depends, of course, on the sensations and inferences. But the senses and inferences persuade me of truth only through the feeling. Each perspective is based on the others and is the basis of the others, which is to say that each perspective is a perspective on the whole.

FOR REVIEW AND REFLECTION

1. "So in an important sense, all knowledge is self-knowledge." Explain, evaluate. Does this mean that we can know nothing outside ourselves?

2. Describe how fallen human beings suppress the truth, and the effect of that on their level of knowledge.
3. "We come to know ourselves by knowing the world." Explain, evaluate. How can this be true if all knowledge is self-knowledge?
4. "There may well be uncharted senses or ESP." Explain, evaluate. Have you had experiences that you would attribute to such uncharted senses?
5. Define "cognitive rest." Have you ever experienced cognitive rest after a period of intellectual uncertainty? Describe this and explain.

GLOSSARY

cognitive rest. The feeling of assurance that comes on us after a period of doubt and inquiry.

existential perspective. The perspective on knowledge that focuses on the self.

intuition. Our initial grasp of data that results in knowledge. Often, when we know something but cannot say how we know it, we say that we know it by intuition.

subjectivity. What goes on within us; our self-knowledge.

FOR FURTHER READING

John Frame, *DKG*. See especially 149–62, 319–46.

Pascal, *Pensées*, available at http://www.ccel.org/ccel/pascal/pensees.html. Many Christian reflections here on the inner dynamics of knowing, especially his famous saying that "the heart has its reasons that reason cannot know."

WHAT TO DO WITH
PERSPECTIVES

IS THERE ANY practical value in all of this? Well, we are after all talking about "theology," and to many, theology is not a very practical discipline. I think, however, that in the most important sense, theology is life. I have defined theology as "the application of Scripture to all areas of human life."[1] I don't think that everyone, even all Christians, are required to study theology as a technical academic discipline. But everyone needs to understand what God's Word requires of us in our daily lives. And in that general theological task, triperspectivalism is a helpful method.

BALANCE

From our discussion of triperspectivalism in this book, it should be evident now that this approach encourages us to look at Scripture as a whole. There are, to be sure, some parts of Scripture that tend to focus on one perspective more than another.

1. For argument to this effect, see chapter 1 of my *ST*.

Let us look, for example, at the OT law and its role in biblical ethics. The OT laws are obviously "normative." The Jewish tradition accepted that there were 613 divine precepts in the Torah or Pentateuch, the first five books of the OT. It would be possible to write these precepts as a list, and that list would serve as a summary of biblical morality.

But that type of morality would not be fully biblical. For the 613 precepts, if that is what they are, are in a context of the redemptive story. God's people are to keep his precepts because he redeemed them from the land of Egypt, the house of slavery (Ex. 20:1). So God's precepts require us to think about the story from which they arise, and that story is a collection of facts that we should list as part of the situational perspective. Often the meaning of the precepts depends on the situational context. The Sabbath commandment, for example (Ex. 20:8–11) is an imitation of God's work of creation (Ex. 20:11) and redemption (Deut. 5:15). The command to keep the Sabbath appears quite arbitrary until we learn the importance of the "seventh day" in the earlier Scripture story.

Indeed, it is the situational context that motivates the people of God to obey his precepts. It is *because* God delivered Israel out of Egypt that Israel should keep God's commands. It is not enough to obey. We should obey for the right reason, from the right motive. So when Jesus expounds the law, as in Matthew 5:1–48, he seeks obedience from the *heart*. It is not enough to avoid literal adultery or murder; the command calls us to a deeper obedience. So we will avoid not only murder but whatever leads to murder, such as anger (verses 21–26). We should abstain not only from literal adultery but also from the lust that tempts us to that sin (verses 27–30).

And God's command also confronts us as *gospel*, the good news of salvation. It is not only the command to be good people but the commandment to believe in Christ: "This is the work of God, that you believe in him whom he has sent" (John 6:29). Only through believing and receiving Christ can we be obedient to God as Jesus is obedient to his Father.

So the situational perspective reaches from outside ourselves to within our hearts. The situational perspective then becomes an existential perspective. We encounter that perspective within our own hearts. But it is not merely "subjective." It is the law itself, the objective law, that requires heart-obedience. So we have not grasped the normative perspective until we perceive within it the existential perspective. The law includes its own applications. And the situational perspective, the biblical story, also generates the existential, our motivation for obedience.

It is thus that Scripture calls us to a balanced view of God's commands. We should not imagine that the law is simply a list of precepts, no matter how many. The law is part of our history, our situation. That history is gospel, the story of God bringing us his way of life and, indeed, of writing his law on our heart. And the gospel changes our hearts so that we can obey God's commands in depth. The normative, situational, and existential perspectives are inseparable. An adequate biblical ethic is not just a list of precepts, nor is it merely a narrative of the gospel. It is a powerful word of the Holy Spirit to the heart.[2]

So it is edifying, when we are doing theology, to go through the perspectives one by one to see if we are missing anything. Have we done justice to the normative? The situational? The existential? We will miss the whole point of biblical ethics if we simply list commandments. The situational story and the existential application are important to the *meaning* of the law. We also miss the point if we try to reduce

2. This discussion speaks to the traditional distinction between law and gospel (see chapter 3), but I shall not explore that here in detail.

the commandments to the story of Jesus. He is the fulfillment of the law, but it is important for us to know how Scripture formulates the laws that Jesus has fulfilled. And we miss the point if we reduce the law to our inward subjectivity or if we reduce inward subjectivity to objective analysis.

SALVATION

When we hear the gospel in this pattern, we see several elements in balance. Referring to the title of John Murray's important book, salvation is "redemption accomplished," the work of Christ in his atonement, ascension, and resurrection, and "redemption applied," the work of God through the Spirit in changing our hearts from within. Redemption accomplished is the situational perspective, and redemption applied the existential. Both of these flow from the normative, the eternal decree of the Father to save all his people from their sins. Like the Trinity, the three of these are not interchangeable. But if one perspective is absent, the others are absent too, and there is no salvation.

So, as I discussed in chapter 3, I do not find it helpful to make a sharp distinction in redemption between objective and subjective.

THE WORD OF GOD

In the doctrine of divine communication, God's Word is normative because it serves as the supreme rule for the conduct of all living beings. It is situational because it is revealed in everything God has made (Ps. 19; Rom. 1:18–21). And it is existential because the Holy Spirit writes it on our hearts (Jer. 31:33), illuminating it and changing our lives (1 Thess. 1:5; 2:13–14).

THE CHRISTIAN LIFE

The Christian life is, in its normative perspective, obeying God's commands. In the situational perspective we *apply* those commands to each situation we encounter. And in the existential perspective, we, through the Spirit, seek to be transformed (Rom. 12:2) by that applied law so that we become living sacrifices to Christ. These aspects of the Christian life are perspectival in the sense that we obey God's commands (normative) only when we apply them to the whole world (situational) from the heart (existential). Insofar as we fail to make these applications from the heart, we have not obeyed God's norms, for they require precisely that application.

PHILOSOPHY

Philosophers are often said to be students of metaphysics, the basic nature of the universe; epistemology, the basic nature of knowledge; and axiology, the theory of value (such as ethics and aesthetics). These three disciplines are perspectivally related. Metaphysics is situational, discussing the ultimate environment that we share with God and creatures. Epistemology is normative, seeking to determine the ultimate criteria of truth and falsity. Axiology is existential, seeking to understand the values by which we live.

But you cannot study any of these disciplines without the others. Axiology (existential) presupposes a normative system of values. To know what is ethically right, for example, you must understand what is true and what is false (the normative). And the reverse is also the case, since truth is a value. To know what is epistemologically true, you must know what is axiologically right. And both of these presuppose metaphysics, for we can know what is right and good only if the world is knowable and our minds are equipped to know it. To say these conditions are true is to have a metaphysical understanding about how the objective world and the subjective mind fit together.

Look also more closely at epistemology, a perspectival subdivision of philosophy. The history of philosophy presents us with three views of how we can attain knowledge: empiricism, through sense experience; rationalism, using rational analysis and logical deduction; and subjectivism, by believing the immediate contents of the mind. But rationalism requires sense experience. Without it we have no data for rational analysis. And empiricism requires rational analysis; otherwise, we do not know what we are seeing and hearing. And both of these presuppose subjectivism: we cannot know the data of the senses or the reason unless they are part of the immediate contents of the mind.

Philosophers tend to resist this perspectival analysis. They would prefer to think that we must choose one, and only one, of these three methods of knowledge. Secular empiricists would like to believe that sense experience *alone* can produce knowledge. The reason is that they have abandoned the idea that God is the key to knowledge. Empiricism is one approach that, taken alone, represents autonomous human thought.

We have seen that when people abandon God, they do not abandon worship (honoring something as ultimate); rather, they worship something other than God and necessarily less than God. Ultimately, they worship themselves. The Bible calls this idolatry. A similar dynamic can be found in epistemology. When people abandon God as the source of knowledge, they do not deny that knowledge needs a source. Rather, they recognize another source as ultimate (sense experience, the power of reason, or immediate subjectivity).

So secular epistemology (like metaphysics and axiology) is idolatry, honoring a false ultimate.

APOLOGETICS

Apologetics is the discipline in which we learn how to answer those who ask us "a reason for the hope that is in you" (1 Peter 3:15). Such questions come from both unbelievers and believers, for believers also often need help in formulating reasons for their hope. Potentially, apologetics can be a useful tool of evangelism. But in practice, much of the apologetics literature is ingrown, with practitioners of one apologetic "method" arguing with those who prefer a different one.

Triperspectivalism, I believe, can help restore unity to apologetics, for much of the arguing, in my opinion, can be traced to a failure to understand how perspectives are interrelated.

The three apologetic methods most frequently under debate are these: (1) Presuppositionalism insists that apologetic arguments be developed in obedience to God's Word, our ultimate presupposition. (2) Evidentialism and classical apologetics emphasize the need to present the gospel as assured facts. (3) Subjectivism urges the hearer to bring his worldview into line with his own deepest beliefs and feelings.

Formulated this way, we can see that presuppositionalism focuses on the normative perspective, evidential / classical on the situational, and subjectivism on the existential. Reconciling these is mainly a matter of understanding how each of these emphases presupposes the other two, how each is actually a perspective on the whole work of apologetics. For each emphasizes one of the epistemological perspectives we considered in the last section: respectively, rationalism, empiricism, and subjectivism.

PEDAGOGY

I've also found triperspectivalism useful in a less philosophical, more practical way. It provides a convenient and memorable way to *teach*. Even apart from Trinitarian doctrine, it seems that the number three rings bells in people's minds. And of course, those bells sometimes summon them to Trinitarian doctrine.

So triperspectivalism provides a series of "hooks" to help students remember teaching content. Since I am mainly a teacher of theology, my triadic hooks look something like this:

- The Trinity: Father, Son, and Spirit
- Divine Lordship: Authority, Control, and Presence
- Divine Attributes: Wisdom, Power, Love
- God's Acts: Decrees, Providence, Salvation
- The Biblical Story: God's Covenants, the Kingdom of God, the Family of God
- Aspects of Covenants: Divine Blessing, Command to Subdue (land), Command to Fill (seed)
- The Word of God: Meaning, Power, Salvation
- Media of the Word: Events, Human Words, Persons
- Human Knowledge: Normative, Situational, Existential
- Man in God's Image: Prophet, King, Priest
- Criteria of Goodness: Standard, Goal, Motive
- Types of Christian Ethics: Command, Narrative, Virtue
- Types of Non-Christian Ethics: Deontological, Teleological, Existential
- Highest Good: Keeping the Commands, New Creation, Faith Working through Love
- Factors in Ethical Judgment: the Word of God, the Situation, the Ethical Agent
- Moral Excellence: Righteousness, Goodness, Holiness

- Sin: Disobedience, Self-Glorification, Hatred
- Effects of the Fall: Guilt, Punishment, Corruption
- Temptation: the Devil, the World, the Flesh
- The Person of Christ: Prophet, King, Priest
- The Work of Christ: His Offices, His States (humiliation/exaltation), Union with Human Beings
- Aspects of Salvation: God's Decree, the Atonement, the Application of Redemption
- The New Creation: Justification, Adoption, Regeneration-Sanctification
- Saving Faith: Belief, Knowledge, and Trust
- Christian Virtues: Faith, Hope, and Love
- Three Aspects of Love: Allegiance, Action, Affection
- Three Aspects of Repentance: Renunciation of Sin, Turning from Sin, Sorrow for Sin
- Means of Sanctification: God's Law, the History of Redemption, Spirit-infused Virtues
- Grounds of Assurance: the Promises of God, Our Growth in Sanctification, the Spirit's Inner Testimony
- The Work of the Church: Worship, the Great Commission, Love
- Aspects of the Great Commission: Divine Blessing, Commands of Christ, Evangelism and Baptism
- Specific Tasks of the Church: Worship, Witness, Nurture
- Characteristics of Worship: Biblical, Christ-Centered, Edifying
- Purposes of Discipline: Instructing the Church, Honoring Christ, Reclaiming the Offender
- Ministries of the Church: Word, Rule, Mercy
- Means of Grace: Word, Fellowship, Prayer
- Reasons to Pray: Divine Command, Prayer Changes Things, Fellowship with God

- Fellowship: Worship, Sharing of Goods, Nurture
- Church Offices: Apostle, Elder, Deacon
- Views of Church Government: Episcopal, Presbyterian, Congregational
- Symbolism of Baptism: Repentance, Cleansing, Union with Christ
- The Lord's Supper: Sign, Seal, Fellowship

For explanations of these, see my *ST*, especially the summary of triads in appendix A. There is a similar appendix in my *DG*, but some of the triads there are a bit speculative and whimsical (e.g., blue, red, and green; height, breadth, and depth).

I am willing to argue that all of the triads above are perspectively related. Take "means of grace" as an example. "Word, fellowship, and prayer"[3] are not sharply separable. When we pray as Scripture warrants, we are applying the Word and we are in fellowship with God. When we read or hear the Word, we are in God's presence, and so we fellowship with him in prayer. And our fellowship is in the Word and in prayer. Since you can't have one of these without the others, the three are perspectively related.

So even people who are skeptical about my general (Trinitarian) argument for triperspectival thinking can profit from triadism as a pedagogical method. But once they profit from that, they may well find the Trinitarian argument more persuasive, that triperspectivalism reflects a deep structure in the biblical worldview.

---

3. The traditional triad is "word, *sacraments*, and prayer." As I explain in *ST*, I have broadened the second category to include not only the sacraments but also other kinds of fellowship.

READING THE BIBLE TRIPERSPECTIVALLY

It is one thing to discuss general concepts in philosophy and theology. For Christians, these are, of course, based on Scripture. But it is another thing to discuss specific biblical texts, the activity scholars call "exegesis." All theology, no matter how general or specific, begins with the exegesis of specific texts. Here I would like to show, through some examples, that triperspectivalism is a help in exegesis as well.

Genesis 1:1–31

The creation story has three notable elements, which can be summarized triperspectivally. (1) It is striking that God's act of creation is an act of language. At each point, the divine speech utters a command. He said, "Let there be light," and there was light (Gen. 1:3). The same happens with each creative act: heaven, earth, vegetation, lights, and so on. This is the normative perspective (see also Ps. 33:6). (2) God's creative word is also a word of power, for when he issues a command, the forces of nature obey him, producing a world full of divinely ordered objects. This is the situational perspective. (3) The climax of creation is God's production of human beings in his image (Gen. 1:26–28). These human beings are to have dominion over all the other creatures, filling the earth and enjoying its blessings. This is the existential perspective: God makes a creature to have subjective enjoyment of all he has made.

Genesis 3:6

When the serpent tempts Eve to disobey God's command and to eat the forbidden fruit, she considers it from three perspectives:

> So when the woman saw that the tree was good for food,
> and that it was a delight to the eyes, and that the tree was to
> be desired to make one wise, she took of its fruit and ate,
> and she also gave some to her husband who was with her,
> and he ate. (Gen. 3:6)

The fruit, she thinks, will nourish her body and give her more strength (situational perspective). It will also provide aesthetic enjoyment to her (existential perspective).[4] And she believes (falsely, of course) that it will give her wisdom that will justify her rebellion against God's command (normative perspective).

Sin is always rebellion against God's lordship: we seek control/power against his control and power. We seek delight apart from God's presence. And we seek wisdom greater than God's. When we draw out the nature of sin perspectivally in this way we can understand better how the three elements fit together, how they cohere in the larger biblical picture of rebellion against God's lordship.

Matthew 4:1–11

This passage is a New Testament parallel to Genesis 3:6. Here Jesus experiences essentially the same temptation that Eve experienced in the earlier passage. The main difference is that Jesus passes the test that Eve failed. We can see that more clearly if we note that in both cases there is a threefold temptation with a triperspectival structure. (1) As with Eve, Jesus is tempted by desire for food (verses 2–4). (2) As Eve was tempted with the prospect of aesthetic delight, Jesus is tempted by the presence of angels to rescue him from falling

---

4. Delight, aesthetic and otherwise, is in Scripture always an adumbration of God's presence.

(verses 5–7), leading to a spectacular display. (3) As Eve sought a wisdom greater than God's, Satan offered Jesus authority over all the nations (verses 8–11). The food temptation is in our terms situational, the falling temptation existential, the authority temptation normative.

1 John 2:16

This passage is also similar to the previous two, presenting a threefold description of sin, as John tells his correspondents not to love "the world":

> For all that is in the world—the desires of the flesh and the desires of the eyes and pride of possessions—is not from the Father but is from the world. (1 John 2:16)

The "desires of the flesh" remind us of the hunger experienced both by Eve and by Jesus. The "desires of the eyes" remind us of Eve's craving for aesthetic pleasure and Jesus' opportunity for spectacular display. The "pride of possessions" recalls Eve's lust for a wisdom greater than God's and Satan's presumption that Jesus would worship him to gain political power over the nations. The three kinds of temptations are all, in different ways, temptations to reject and even replace the authority of God's lordship. For only God can supply our physical hungers, our desire for visible stimulation, and our craving for authority.

Ephesians 1:15–23

Let us now consider Paul's prayer for the Ephesian Christians:

> For this reason, because I have heard of your faith in the Lord Jesus and your love toward all the saints, I do

not cease to give thanks for you, remembering you in my prayers, that the God of our Lord Jesus Christ, the Father of glory, may give you the a spirit of wisdom and of revelation in the knowledge of him, having the eyes of your hearts enlightened, that you may know what is the hope to which he has called you, what are the riches of his glorious inheritance in the saints, and what is the immeasurable greatness of his power toward us who believe, according to the working of his great might that he worked in Christ when he raised him from the dead and seated him at his right hand in the heavenly places, far above all rule and authority and power and dominion, and above every name that is named, not only in this age but also in the one to come. And he put all things under his feet and gave him as head over all things to the church, which is his body, the fullness of him who fills all in all. (Ephesians 1:15–23)

Note the Trinitarian structure of this passage: Paul speaks of God the Father ("the God of our Lord Jesus Christ"), Christ himself, and the Holy Spirit as the gift of the Father and Son. The themes of control/power (verse 19), authority (verse 21), and presence (verses 22–23) suffuse the text.

Not every passage can be analyzed into a triad. But a surprising number of them can be. When we are alert to such patterns in our Bible reading, we are reminded of something very important—that the word of God aims to exalt, to glorify God's lordship in our lives. It is not surprising that whether these passages are read by themselves or whether they are brought together into the categories of systematic theology and Christian philosophy, they focus like a laser on God's control, authority, and presence, his lordship over us and all things.

A TRIPERSPECTIVAL MANDATE

Some may be looking now for a "bottom line." Is trip-erspectivalism merely an abstract theological theory with no concrete practical relevance? Or is there something in this approach that can change our lives?

I think the latter is true. The fundamental teaching of Scripture is that God is *Lord*. The various Hebrew and Greek terms translated *Lord* are over 7,000 in number. "God is the Lord" is the theme of the Old Testament; "Jesus Christ is Lord" is the theme of the New.

Let us consider first the Old Testament. In Exodus 3, Moses asks what he should reply when the Israelites ask the name of God. God replies,

> "Say this to the people of Israel, 'The LORD, the God of your fathers, the God of Abraham, the God of Isaac, and the God of Jacob, has sent me to you.' This is my name forever, and thus I am to be remembered throughout all generations." (Ex. 3:15)

Here, God promises to deliver Israel from their slavery in Egypt. And here is the purpose of that deliverance:

> "I will take you to be my people, and I will be your God, and you shall know that I am the LORD your God, who has brought you out from under the burdens of the Egyptians." (Ex. 6:7)

Israel was groaning under their bondage. Deliverance would make them free. But the greatest blessing of this deliverance was their new relation to God: they were to be his people, and he was to be their God. This was a blessing beyond the blessings experienced by any other nation. And there is more: "You shall know that I am the LORD your God." Israel's blessing is fundamentally God-centered.

The name *Yahweh*, Lord, that God revealed to Moses is highly mysterious. It seems to be related to the Hebrew verb "to be," but in what way? Exegesis only deepens the mystery. But God chooses to reveal the mystery to some extent by his actions, by his deliverance of Israel. One major function of the deliverance is to reveal the divine name. He wants Israel to *know that I am the Lord.*

At other important points in the narrative as well, God does this or that so that people can know that he is the Lord. The Egyptians, too, receive such revelation: "The Egyptians shall know that I am the LORD, when I stretch out my hand against Egypt and bring out the people of Israel from among them." (Ex. 7:5) The salvation of Israel, as well as the defeat of Egypt, is a revelation of God's lordship. This is a pervasive theme of the exodus story. (See also Ex. 7:17; 8:10, 22; 9:29; 10:2; 14:4, 18; 16:6, 12; 29:46; 31:13.) Whatever God does for Israel, he does so that they may know that he is the Lord.

The exodus story is the Old Testament gospel. It tells how God delivered Israel from bondage and brought them (through sinful episodes) into the land he promised to Abraham. In this gospel, God identifies himself as the Lord. Earlier in this book I explained lordship in terms of God's "lordship attributes." So here, he displays his *control* over all the forces of nature, his *authority* to command his people and the Egyptians as well, and his *presence* as he dwells in and with Israel, so that he might be their God and they his people.

Now consider the New Testament. The Old Testament promises another deliverance, greater than the deliverance of Israel from Egypt. The new deliverance centers on a "servant of the Lord" who will redeem not only Israel but the other nations as well. Isaiah proclaims,

> Behold my servant, whom I uphold, my chosen, in whom my soul delights; I have put my Spirit upon him; he will bring forth justice to the nations. He will not cry aloud or lift up his voice, or make it heard in the street; a bruised reed he will not break, and a faintly burning wick he will not quench; he will faithfully bring forth justice. He will not grow faint or be discouraged till he has established justice in the earth; and the coastlands wait for his law. (Isa. 42:1–4)

But the new deliverance is not only the coming of a servant of God; it is the coming of God himself:

> But now thus says the LORD, he who created you, O Jacob, he who formed you, O Israel: "Fear not, for I have redeemed you; I have called you by name, you are mine. When you pass through the waters, I will be with you; and through the rivers, they shall not overwhelm you; when you walk through fire you shall not be burned, and the flame shall not consume you. For I am the LORD your God, the Holy One of Israel, your Savior. I give Egypt as your ransom, Cush and Seba in exchange for you. Because you are precious in my eyes, and honored, and I love you, I give men in return for you, peoples in exchange for your life." (Isa. 43:1–4)

> "You are my witnesses," declares the LORD, "and my servant whom I have chosen, that you may know and believe me and understand that I am he. Before me no god was formed, nor shall there be any after me. I, I am the LORD, and besides

me there is no savior. I declared and saved and proclaimed, when there was no strange god among you; and you are my witnesses," declares the LORD, "and I am God. Also henceforth I am he; there is none who can deliver from my hand; I work, and who can turn it back?" (Isa. 43:10–13)

The "I am he" refers back to the divine name Yahweh, "I am," the Lord. These passages speak richly of his lordship attributes. By his control, he delivers Israel from waters and fires. He works, and nobody can turn it back. By his authority, he declares and proclaims his salvation. He calls Israel by name. By his presence, he proclaims that he will be *with* Israel as they go through the threatening waters.

So the promise is the coming of a messenger and of the Lord himself:

> "Behold, I send my messenger, and he will prepare the way before me. And the Lord whom you seek will suddenly come to his temple; and the messenger of the covenant in whom you delight, behold, he is coming, says the LORD of hosts." (Mal. 3:1)

The message of the New Testament is that this messenger-servant has come in Jesus Christ. But Jesus Christ is not merely a representative of God; he is God himself. He is Lord. Of Jesus, Paul says,

> Therefore God has highly exalted him and bestowed on him the name that is above every name, so that at the name of Jesus every knee should bow, in heaven and on earth and under the earth, and every tongue confess that Jesus Christ is Lord, to the glory of God the Father. (Phil. 2:9–11; see also Rom. 10:9; 1 Cor. 12:3)

The fundamental confession of the New Testament gospel is "Jesus Christ is Lord." It is in Jesus Christ that God finally informs us what it means for him to be Lord.

By his control, Jesus destroys the power of Satan and draws us to himself. By his authority, Jesus speaks as the Word of God (John 1:1–14). By his presence, he speaks to us as Yahweh spoke to Israel: "And behold, I am with you always, to the end of the age" (Matt. 28:20).

The significance of triperspectivalism is that it keeps us focused on the biblical bottom line, that God is nothing less than the Lord, and that his lordship is fully revealed in Jesus Christ. The most fundamental element of the gospel is Jesus, not the distinctives of the various denominations and historical traditions; not this creed or that creed, this confession or that confession; not this emphasis or that emphasis, this method or that method; not this liturgy or that liturgy. It is not even the particular doctrines that constitute together the overall content of systematic theology. Jesus himself is our creator, our redeemer, our prophet, priest, and king. So everything we do as Christians should be done to Jesus as Lord.

FOR REVIEW AND REFLECTION

1. Share an experience in which you have seen theology "come to life" for you in an application to your life.
2. Give an example of how a triperspectival approach might encourage more balance in the application of Scripture.
3. How is the Word of God triperspectival? Explain.
4. Discuss triperspectivally the relation between metaphysics, epistemology, and axiology.
5. Does triperspectivalism minimize the differences

between the different schools of apologetics? Why or why not?

6. Are there some threefold distinctions listed under pedagogy that strike you as useful in communicating the gospel? Show why they are useful. Or if none of them are useful, explain why.

7. Are there Bible passages that you think can be usefully expounded from a triperspectival approach? Describe one or two of these, and share how you think the three perspectives can help you to understand or communicate them.

8. "The significance of triperspectivalism is that it keeps us focused on the biblical bottom line, that God is nothing less than the Lord, and that his lordship is fully revealed in Jesus Christ." Explain, evaluate.

GLOSSARY

apologetics. The discipline in which we learn how to answer those who ask us "a reason for the hope that is in you" (1 Peter 3:15).

axiology. The philosophical discipline that studies the nature of value.

classical apologetics. A school of apologetics that emphasizes proofs for the existence of God and evidences of biblical history.

epistemology. The philosophical discipline that studies the nature of knowledge.

evidentialism. A school of apologetics that emphasizes the need to present the gospel as assured facts.

exegesis. Study of specific biblical texts.

metaphysics. The philosophical discipline that explores the nature and basic structure of the universe.

presuppositionalism. The school of apologetics that emphasizes the normative perspective and stresses the importance of developing arguments that are in accord with God's Word as our ultimate presupposition.

subjectivism. A school of apologetics that urges the inquirer to bring his worldview into line with his deepest beliefs and feelings.

theology. The application of Scripture to all areas of human life.

Yahweh. Hebrew name of God, related to the verb "to be," generally translated *Lord* in English Bibles.

FOR FURTHER READING

John Frame, *ST*. I have developed my systematics, and my other lordship books, to show that the center of theology in the Bible is the lordship of God and specifically of Jesus Christ.

GLOSSARY

apologetics. The discipline in which we learn how to answer those who ask us "a reason for the hope that is in you" (1 Peter 3:15).

attribute. A quality or predicate of something. The attributes of God are his perfections.

authority. The lordship attribute of God by which he has the right to be obeyed in everything he commands.

autonomous. Thinking or acting without accepting any standard from outside ourselves.

axiology. The philosophical discipline that studies the nature of value.

circumcessio. The doctrine that the Father, Son, and Holy Spirit are "in" one another. Synonymous with *Circumincessio, perichoresis*.

classical apologetics. A school of apologetics that emphasizes proofs for the existence of God and evidences of biblical history.

cognitive rest. The feeling of assurance that comes on us after a period of doubt and inquiry.

control. The lordship attribute of God indicating his power to determine all the events of nature and history.

criterion. A standard for judging the nature of something or the truth of a statement.

emotion, or **feeling**. That aspect of the human mind associated with self-awareness.

empiricism. The philosophical theory that human sense experience is the ultimate criterion of knowledge and truth.

epistemology. The philosophical discipline that studies the nature of knowledge.

evidence. Alleged facts adduced to prove or verify a conclusion.

evidentialism. A school of apologetics that emphasizes the need to present the gospel as assured facts.

exegesis. Study of specific biblical texts.

existential perspective. A perspective of human knowledge, focusing on our internal subjective experience in close proximity to God's presence.

facts. States of affairs, objects of knowledge. A component of the situational perspective. Facts thought to be separate from any interpretative activity.

filioque. Term added to the Nicene Creed in the Western church, indicating that the Holy Spirit proceeds from the Father *and the Son*, not from the Father only. *Filioque* means "and the Son."

forms. The qualities that make everything what it is. In Plato's philosophy, forms exist in a realm distinct from the world of our experience.

gospel. Good news, particularly the news that God has brought salvation to those who trust in Jesus.

grace. God's unmerited favor to those who deserve his wrath.

history. The series of events in time that is significant for human life and particularly for human salvation.

intellect. That aspect of the mind associated with knowing.

intuition. Our initial grasp of data that results in knowledge. Often, when we know something but cannot say how we know it, we say that we know it by intuition.

king. One appointed by God to rule over and subdue a nation to God's obedience. One of the "three offices" of Jesus.

knowledge. Ability to act appropriately in regard to facts, norms, and/or the inner life.

law. The rules or norms that define obedience to God.

lordship attributes. God's attributes of control, authority, and presence, which in Scripture define the nature of God's lordship.

metaphysics. The philosophical discipline that explores the nature and basic structure of the universe.

naturalistic fallacy. G. E. Moore's term for arguments that begin with factual (non-normative) premises and seek to derive normative conclusions. Reasoning from "is" to "ought." An argument that fails to justify its normative conclusions.

normative perspective. A perspective of knowledge in which we focus on the world as a revelation of God's will.

norms. What God requires of us. Obligations. What *ought* to be the case.

objective. Divinely established as fact, regardless of what creatures would prefer to believe.

omniperspectival. God's omniscience, understood as his ability to understand everything from every possible perspective.

omniscience. God's attribute of knowing everything.

personal properties. Qualities of the three Trinitarian persons that they do not share with one another. The Father has the property of eternally begetting the Son, the Son the property of being eternally begotten by the Father, and the Spirit the property of proceeding from the Father and the Son. (But see *filioque*.)

personal. Able to know, think, plan, communicate verbally, etc.

perspective. A view of something by someone from somewhere.

pou sto. A place to stand (Archimedes). The starting point of an inquiry or endeavor, which gives insight and power.

presence. The lordship attribute by which God is present to everything in the world.

presuppositionalism. The school of apologetics that emphasizes the normative perspective and stresses the importance of developing arguments that are in accord with God's Word as our ultimate presupposition.

priest. One appointed by God to bring sacrifice to him and to intercede for his people. One of the "three offices" of Jesus.

primacy of the intellect. The theory that truth comes first into the intellect and thereafter to the will and emotions. The theory often asserts that the intellect should be more central than the will and emotions to human decision making.

prophet. One appointed by God to set forth the word of God infallibly. One of the "three offices" of Jesus.

qualitative difference. A difference in kind, not just quantity. One way to indicate the vastness of the difference between God's thoughts and our own.

rationalism. The philosophical view that human reason is the ultimate source of knowledge.

redemption. God's gracious acts to restore fallen human beings through the atonement of Christ.

regeneration. The new birth, in which the Holy Spirit creates in us a new heart of faith and obedience (John 3:3).

revelation. Knowledge given by a source outside ourselves, particularly by God. See definitions in text of "general," "special," and "existential" revelation.

ring of truth. Our ability to judge the truth of a statement by way of our God-given intuition of what truth sounds like.

Sabellianism. The heretical view that God is only one person who plays the roles of Father, Son, and Holy Spirit.

sacred. The sphere of God's holiness.

sanctification. The work of the Holy Spirit by which sinners are made holy.

secular. That which is not holy, but common or profane.

simplicity. God's quality of having no parts. His attributes are not parts of him but perspectives on his whole being; for example, God's love is God.

situational perspective. A perspective of knowledge in which we focus on the objects in the world.

subjective/subjectivity. Existing in the human consciousness, mind, or feelings.

subjectivism. A school of apologetics that urges the inquirer to bring his worldview into line with his deepest beliefs and feelings.

theology. The application of Scripture to all areas of human life.

Trinity. The Christian doctrine that there is one God in three persons, Father, Son, and Holy Spirit.

two kingdoms. The distinction between the sacred and the secular, according to some theologians.

will. That aspect of the mind associated with choosing.

works. Actions performed by persons, which in some cases are thought to merit reward.

Yahweh. Divine name revealed to Moses in Exodus 3:15, generally translated *Lord* in English Bibles; related to the verb "to be."

BIBLIOGRAPHY

Augustine, *On the Trinity*. 2nd ed. In *Works of Saint Augustine: A Translation for the 21st Century*. Translated by Edmund Hill. Edited by John E. Rotelle. Hyde Park, NY: New City Press, 2012.

Frame, John M. *Apologetics: A Justification of Christian Belief*. Phillipsburg, NJ: P&R Publishing, 2015.

———. *A Theology of Lordship*. 4 vols. Phillipsburg, NJ: P&R Publishing, 1987–2010.

———. *Cornelius Van Til: An Analysis of His Thought*. Phillipsburg, NJ: P&R Publishing, 1995.

———. *The Doctrine of the Christian Life*. A Theology of Lordship, vol. 3. Phillipsburg, NJ: P&R Publishing, 2008.

———. *The Doctrine of God*. A Theology of Lordship, vol. 2. Phillipsburg, NJ: P&R Publishing, 2002.

———. *The Doctrine of the Knowledge of God*. A Theology of Lordship, vol. 1. Phillipsburg, NJ: Presbyterian and Reformed, 1987.

———. *The Doctrine of the Word of God*. A Theology of Lordship, vol. 4. Phillipsburg, NJ: P&R Publishing, 2010.

———. *The Escondido Theology*. Lakeland, FL: Whitefield Media Productions, 2011.

———. *A History of Western Philosophy and Theology*. Phillipsburg, NJ: P&R Publishing, 2015.

————. *Perspectives on the Word of God.* Eugene, OR: Wipf & Stock, 1999.

————. *Selected Shorter Writings, Vol. 1.* Phillipsburg, NJ: P&R Publishing, 2014.

————. *Selected Shorter Writings, Vol. 2.* Phillipsburg, NJ: P&R Publishing, 2015.

————. *Selected Shorter Writings, Vol. 3.* Phillipsburg, NJ: P&R Publishing, 2016.

————. *Systematic Theology: An Introduction to Christian Belief.* Phillipsburg, NJ: P&R Publishing, 2013.

Murray, John. *Redemption Accomplished and Applied.* Grand Rapids: Eerdmans, 1955.

Pascal, Blaise. *Pensées.* Christian Classics Ethereal Library. http://www.ccel.org/ccel/pascal/pensees.html.

Poythress, Vern S. *The Lordship of Christ: Serving Our Savior All of the Time, in All of Life, with All of Our Heart.* Wheaton, IL: Crossway, 2016.

————. *Knowing and the Trinity: How Perspectives in Human Knowledge Imitate the Trinity.* Phillipsburg, NJ: P&R Publishing, 2018.

————. *Philosophy, Science and the Sovereignty of God.* Nutley, NJ: Presbyterian and Reformed, 1976.

————. *Redeeming Mathematics: A God-Centered Approach.* Wheaton, IL: Crossway, 2015.

————. *Redeeming Philosophy: A God-Centered Approach.* Wheaton, IL: Crossway, 2016.

————. *Redeeming Science: A God-Centered Approach.* Wheaton, IL: Crossway, 2006.

————. *Redeeming Sociology: A God-Centered Approach.* Wheaton, IL: Crossway, 2011.

————. "Reforming Ontology and Logic in the Light of the Trinity," *Westminster Theological Journal* 57, 1 (1995), 187–219.

————. *Symphonic Theology: The Validity of Multiple Perspectives in Theology.* Grand Rapids: Zondervan, 1987.

Van Til, Cornelius. *Christian Theistic Ethics*. In Defense of Biblical Christianity, vol. 3. https://presupp101.files.wordpress.com /2011/08/van-til-christian-theistic-ethics.pdf.

———. *A Christian Theory of Knowledge*. Nutley, NJ: Presbyterian and Reformed, 1969.

———. *A Survey of Christian Epistemology*. Philadelphia: Den Dulk Christian Foundation, 1969.

Warfield, B. B. "The Biblical Doctrine of the Trinity." In *The Works of Benjamin B. Warfield*. 10 vols. New York: Oxford University Press, 1927–32. Reprint, Grand Rapids: Baker, 1991.

INDEX OF SCRIPTURE

INDEX OF SUBJECTS AND NAMES

ALSO BY JOHN M. FRAME

Systematic Theology is the culmination and creative synthesis of John Frame's writing on, teaching about, and studying of the Word of God. This magisterial opus—at once biblical, clear, cogent, readable, accessible, and practical—summarizes the mature thought of one of the most important and original Reformed theologians of the last hundred years. It will enable you to see clearly how the Bible explains God's great, sweeping plan for mankind.

"This is a remarkable volume—a wonderfully clear, refreshingly insightful, profoundly biblical treatment of systematic theology. While reading this book, I felt as though I once again had the privilege of being a student in John Frame's theology classes, the classes that so deeply influenced my thinking as a Westminster Seminary student forty years ago. But now the material has been enriched by a lifetime of further research and teaching. An outstanding achievement!"
   —Wayne Grudem

ALSO BY JOHN M. FRAME

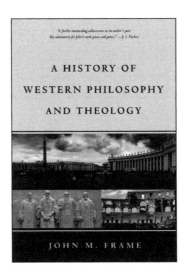

**Winner of the 2017 ECPA Gold Medallion Award
in the Bible Reference Works Category**

A History of Western Philosophy and Theology is the fruit of John Frame's forty-five years of teaching philosophical subjects. No other survey of the history of Western thought offers the same invigorating blend of expositional clarity, critical insight, and biblical wisdom. The supplemental study questions, bibliographies, links to audio lectures, quotes from influential thinkers, twenty appendices, and indexed glossary make this an excellent main textbook choice for seminary- and college-level courses and for personal study.

"This is the most important book ever written on the major figures and movements in philosophy. We have needed a sound guide, and this is it."
    —Vern S. Poythress

ALSO BY JOHN M. FRAME

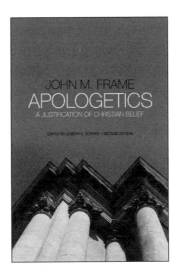

In this extensively redeveloped and expanded version of *Apologetics to the Glory of God* (1994), renowned theologian John Frame sheds light on the message and method of genuinely Christian apologetics in terms of proof, defense, and offense.

"John Frame's *Apologetics to the Glory of God* brought about a paradigm shift . . . in my understanding not only of apologetics but of all other intellectual endeavors as a Christian. Ever since then, it has been the first book I recommend to those looking for an introduction to Christian apologetics."
   —James N. Anderson

"John Frame winsomely, patiently, and persuasively contends for the gospel and brings together a rare blend of big-picture thinking, level-headed reflection, biblical fidelity, love for the gospel and the church, and ability to write with care and clarity."
   —John Piper